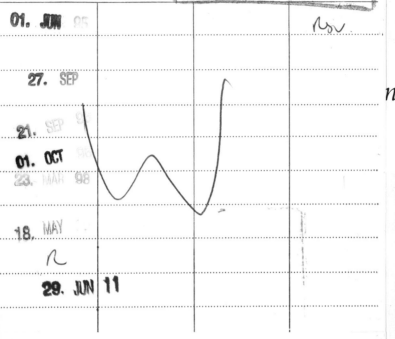

KT-168-579

ng

SMITH, C. *LAVETT*
Fish Watching: An Outdoor Guide to
Freshwater Fishes.

CLASS NO. 597.092 SMI

TO AVOID FINES THIS BOOK SHOULD BE RETURNED ON
OR BEFORE THE LAST DATE STAMPED ABOVE, IF NOT
REQUIRED BY ANOTHER READER IT MAY BE RENEWED BY
PERSONAL CALL, TELEPHONE OR POST, QUOTING THE
DETAILS DISPLAYED.

Fish

An Outdoor Guide

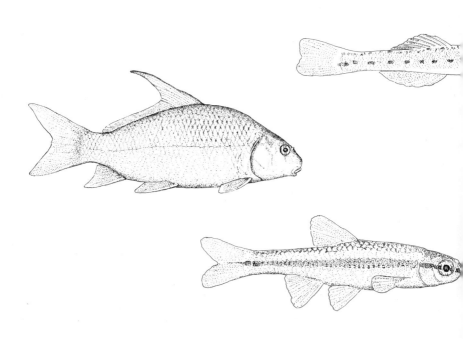

Comstock Publishing Associates

Watching

to Freshwater Fishes

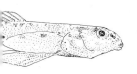

C. LAVETT SMITH

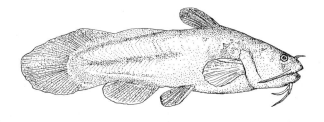

a division of CORNELL UNIVERSITY PRESS

Ithaca and London

First published 1994 by Cornell University Press.

Printed in the United States of America.

Color plates printed in Hong Kong.

⊗ The paper in this book meets the minimum requirements of the
American National Standard for Information Sciences—Permanence
of Paper for Printed Library Materials, ANSI Z39.48-1984.

Library of Congress Cataloging-in-Publication Data

Smith, C. Lavett, 1927–
    Fish watching : an outdoor guide to freshwater fishes / C. Lavett
  Smith.
       p.   cm.
    Includes bibliographical references (p.   ) and index.
    ISBN 0-8014-2827-0 (cloth). — ISBN 0-8014-8084-1 (paper)
    1. Fish watching—United States.   2. Fish watching—Canada.
  3. Freshwater fishes—United States.   4. Freshwater fishes—Canada.
  I. Title.
  QL627.S625   1994
  597.092'973—dc20   93-37112

Contents

The color plates follow page 180.

Acknowledgments

So many people have taught me about fishes that it is impossible to thank them all individually, but a few stand out because they shaped my outlook and taught me to really enjoy fishes. The late Edward Raney of Cornell University introduced me to fishes, and Robert Zilliox of the New York State Conservation Department, also deceased, guided me through my first season as a fisheries professional. At Tulane University, Royal Suttkus and the late Frederick Cagle guided a great group of us graduate students. Allen Chaney, Ernest Liner, Paul Anderson, and Richard Etheridge have gone on to distinguished teaching and research careers. At the University of Michigan, Reeve M. Bailey showed me the kind of scientist and human being I wanted to be. Robert Rush Miller and my fellow graduate students Howard Winn, Carter Gilbert, Carroll Norden, Jack Schultz, and Gerald Smith were especially influential in those formative years. Claude Hibbard introduced me to another dimension, fossil fishes and paleontological fieldwork.

At the American Museum of Natural History, Donn Rosen, Gareth Nelson, James Atz, Carl Ferraris, and Melanie Stiassny have guided and inspired me. Two outstanding volunteers, Irwin A. Levy and Sol Heiligman, have aided this project in many ways.

The best teachers of all have been my students. Generations of students at field stations have shown me what is interesting about fishes, and Amelia Janisz, George Dale, Jerry L. Platt, Chang-Hua Chang, John Waldman, Felix Locicero, Loretta Stillman, Braxton

Dew, Wilbur Curless, and Helena Andreyko have kept the spark alive. James Tyler has guided me in many parts of the world, and my colleagues Robert Daniels, Carl George, Thomas R. Lake, Charles Keene, and Robert Schmidt have shared my enthusiasm for the fishes of New York State. Finally, it is such people as Thomas Lake, Christopher Letts, and Robert Boyle, whose love of the Hudson River and its fishes never dims, who have made this effort worthwhile.

The exquisite habitat drawings are the work of Ruth Soffer and the superb photographs of the sculpin, johnny darter, and variegate darter are by Raymond A. Mendez. The book's final form is due to the professionalism of the editorial and production staff of Cornell University Press. I am especially indebted to Barbara H. Salazar, whose meticulous copy editing made me feel I should go back and take fourth-grade English over again.

C. L. S.

Fish Watching

1 A Land of Fishes

North America is truly a land of water, one richly endowed with varied aquatic habitats. In much of the land west of the Mississippi, streams with their precious supply of water thin out, but the East sustains nearly the full range of aquatic microcosms, from tiny bog ponds to the Great Lakes. Streams range from tiny creeks to the huge Mississippi River, which, with its tributaries, drains about a third of the continent. There are torrential streams and sluggish streams, brown waters and white waters, clear brooks and muddy rivers.

Some of the best sport fishing in the world is to be found in the Eastern United States. A perusal of the records list of the International Game Fish Association reveals a large number of world record fish taken from streams and reservoirs of the area. These waters once supported thriving commercial fisheries, but the industry has dwindled as some species have been overfished, others have become more valuable as sport fish, and pollution has rendered some stocks hazardous to human health.

A few industries dependent on fishes have simply failed to survive in the modern world. In the early part of the twentieth century the Mohawk River in upstate New York was the site of a fishery for eels, whose skins were used to wrap the handles of buggy whips. This trade seems unlikely to be revived.

North Americans have always taken their fishing seriously. One of the first public corporations in North America was a commercial fishing company organized when New York was New Amsterdam. Attempts to improve, manage, and preserve our fishery resources span the entire history of fishery science. The earliest attempts to improve fishing consisted of the introduction of species from the Old World. Common carp were introduced into New York State near Newburgh in 1832; goldfish had probably been introduced somewhat earlier. They were soon followed by brown trout from Europe and rainbow trout from the western United States. In the late nineteenth century and early twentieth a great variety of fishes were introduced into eastern waters from other parts of North America as well as from overseas.

Today we are more careful about introducing exotic wildlife. Sanctioned introductions now are made only after exhaustive consideration of the potential adverse effects on the native species and the environment in general. Even then, the newcomer may become a pest. And despite precautions, aquarium fishes escape and foreign organisms are carried to our shores in cargo ships' ballast water.

Aquatic resources, especially but not exclusively fishes, have come to play important roles in the resolution of larger environmental problems. Outstanding examples are the power plant controversies that led to the landmark Hudson River settlement agreement executed in 1981, and the Westway case, in which protection of the winter habitat of young striped bass became a central issue in a legal decision that led to the abandonment of plans to build a major highway along the west side of Manhattan island, at an estimated cost of $42,000 per lineal inch.

What This Book Is About

This book is about fishes—what they are, where and how they live, what they look like, and how you can see them in their natural habitats. Perhaps even more important, I hope to show you why you should care about fish and to persuade you that time spent watching them is rewarding.

To some people, fish are good for nothing but catching or eating, but there is really much more to fish than the pleasure of the chase and their value as a source of high-quality protein. Fishes are a necessary part of our environment. During the past couple of decades millions of people have come to realize that our planet is in danger and have dedicated their energies to protecting and improving the world we live in. I am reminded of a dialogue in an old *Pogo* comic strip which starts when one of the characters says that "everyone is talking about it." "I'm not talking about it."

"You're not everyone."

"No, but without me, no one is everyone."

This is the way it is with our environment: nothing in it is really expendable.

It is now fashionable to be concerned about maintaining "biodiversity," by which we mean keeping alive in the wild as many species as we possibly can. Many of the forms that make up the world's fauna are rare, some so rare that they are known only from a single specimen in some museum. What is so important about protecting these rare species? In the first place, a rare species represents a gap in our knowledge. Is it really rare or does it thrive in a habitat that we haven't identified or haven't been able to sample efficiently? It it is rare, has it always been so, or have we somehow altered its habitat so that it can no longer thrive there? In the latter case, precisely what is it that we have done to the habitat and how can we prevent the same kinds of disasters from happening to other special habitats? If its rarity is due to our failure to discover its habitat, what other surprises await us there?

Every species is unique. It is unique in its genetic makeup, in its structure, and in the way it manages to survive in the competitive world of nature. To lose any element is to destroy the completeness of our world, to rob us of a potentially beneficial organism, and to make our environment poorer. In a larger sense there is more to biodiversity than simple species lists. Not only is each species unique but so is each phase of its life history, so that every species represents a distinctive set of solutions to the common environmental problems faced by all living things.

Fishes belong here as much as we do. About half the vertebrates in the world are fishes; that is, there are as many kinds of fishes as of birds, mammals, reptiles, and amphibians combined. This alone is reason enough not to ignore them, but the real incentive for learning about fish is simply that they are fascinating.

For more than a third of a century I have been lucky enough to make my living as an ichthyologist—a student of fishes. It's a wonderful profession because each day I learn something new, and the thrill of discovery never dims. But the best part of an ichthyologist's life is the fieldwork. In the field we meet the fishes on their own terms and let them tell us how they live.

It has taken me a long time to learn to watch fishes, and I'm still a beginner in comparison with a lot of anglers. I envy the depth of their knowledge and understanding. Still, my own work has given me a chance to sample the fish world in library, laboratory, and the waters of many parts of the globe.

This book is a spin-off of fieldwork done in connection with work on the inland fishes of New York State. It is not intended to be either a textbook or an identification manual. Rather, it is an effort to tell you how and where to watch fishes and to give you enough background so that you too can get all excited about watching a bullhead herding its young or a gar stalking its prey. Although this book focuses on the northeastern United States, it will be useful throughout the United States and Canada east of the Rocky Mountains. Many of our freshwater fishes have extensive geographical ranges, and all of the families that are native to fresh water east of the Rockies are included.

"All About Fish"

Every once in awhile you will run into an angler who is ready to admit that he knows "all about fish." Why, he can recognize maybe forty or fifty kinds of fish and probably can name even more. "Let's see now, there's bass and pike and perch and bluegills, walleye and catfish and salmon and smelt and . . ." The angler is, of course, naming the species that are of most interest to him, for catching or for eating. A lot of anglers are vaguely aware that there are a few other fish around, but they're just trash fish or "minnies," or forage for the important species. Sometimes they get on a hook accidentally or make nuisances of themselves by stealing the bait, and the sooner "the state" gets rid of them, the better. The real loser here is the angler, who is missing some of the best parts of his hobby.

Of course not all anglers have this attitude. Many are excellent observers with a genuine interest in their prey and everything else about the out-of-doors. Still, most anglers are surprised to learn that there are some 790 kinds of fishes in the fresh waters of North America (167 in New York alone) and that the American Fisheries Society's list of freshwater and marine fishes out to the 100-fathom line includes 2,268 species of the United States and Canada. Furthermore, many species vary recognizably from place to place in their geographic ranges. You can tell a northern pearl dace from an Allegheny pearl dace with some confidence, although you have to take a close look and maybe count a few scales to be sure. Thus the fauna is even more diverse than the species count alone would indicate. When you consider that each species has its own unique genetic makeup, its own distinctive way of life, its own life history, and its own destiny, it becomes apparent that the fishes are worth knowing better.

"Nongame" Fishes

Fishes that are not valued by sport anglers are collectively, and sometimes derisively, called nongame species. Some, such as the darters (small members of the perch family), are among the most colorful fishes in the world. Minnows, members of the family *Cyprinidae*, can also be quite colorful during their breeding season, and you will look at a lot of fish before you find one prettier than a male longear sunfish in full color.

True, some of our species are rather somber, and when they are not in their breeding frippery a lot of minnows may look so much alike that it is almost a case of "If you've seen one, you've seen them all." Even well-trained fishery biologists are apt to lump some of them together as "little silvery bastards." But such similarity is a red flag to ecologists, who immediately wonder how the species manage to live together. Are their habits as similar as their appearance? How do they share food and space in their natural habitats? In fact, do they really live together, or are they separated on some very small scale? How do they recognize potential mates and how do they tell each other apart? These are significant questions indeed, for they hold the keys to the workings of natural communities. They also tell us a great deal about the capacity of the vertebrate brain, and so they help us to understand ourselves a little better.

Perhaps the greatest fascination of fishes is the variety of interesting things they do. Not only do they select their habitats carefully and precisely, but each species has its own way of making a living. Food habits, for instance, are surprisingly varied. Sunfishes are generalized predators on insects and other small bottom-dwelling invertebrates. The stoneroller scrapes algae off rocks. Shad and alewives strain plant and animal plankton from open waters; golden shiners chase down individual plankters one by one. Pikes and pickerels are highly specialized for feeding on other fishes.

Breeding habits are similarly varied. Carp and goldfish simply broadcast their eggs over vegetation or gravel. Sunfishes scrape out shallow bowl-shaped nests, and the fallfish and river chub gather great piles of pebbles so that their nests look as if someone had dumped wheelbarrow loads of gravel in the stream. Catfishes guard their nests and young; suckers simply abandon the eggs. Lampreys and Pacific salmon die soon after spawning. Sturgeon may reproduce for more than 50 years, although they spawn only about once every three years. Common shiners are gregarious and travel in schools; largemouth bass are essentially hermits until mating time. Rainbow trout are wanderers; johnny darters probably spend their entire lives in a few square feet.

Sport fishers, the successful ones at least, devote a great deal of effort to learning the habits of their quarries. They know where the fish are at each season, the depths and temperatures the fish prefer, and when they are most likely to be feeding. They know what kind of bait to use and how to present it to the fish. By extending these kinds of observations to other species, whether we want to catch them or just to watch them, we can gain a great understanding of natural ecosystems.

Our big challenge is to find patterns in nature. Aquatic systems are especially good places to start because they are so different from our own environment that we are not so tempted to take any aspect of them for granted. We can view each aquatic system as a whole and then try to find and analyze its natural subdivisions. We can try to discover the special place that each species occupies in the system and then we can see how small differences between the species enable each one to use the environment in a unique way, thus allowing it to share the available resources with its neighbors.

How to Use This Book

This book is intended to be used in the field, so after a few preliminaries we start the main text with habitat. When you come to a body of water that looks interesting to you, you can readily find a section in the book that will give you some guidance as to what to look for and what you may expect to find.

Unfortunately, the fishes themselves have not taken this approach very seriously. Thus you will find trout in headwater streams, mid-reach streams, base-level streams, large rivers, ponds, and large lakes. You will find perches in small streams and in large lakes. For this reason each section begins with a general discussion of the habitat and its subdivisions ("microhabitats"). Then the fishes that may be expected to live in that type of habitat are introduced.

Sometimes you will find yourself wanting to know more about the fish you see. What are they? What are they related to and where else in the world do their relatives live? What is their lifestyle? Answers to such questions can be sought in three additional places: general accounts of the families are found in chapter 4, sections on selected aspects of fish biology and ecology appear in chapter 5, and appendix 1 provides a general overview of the relationships of fishes. Finally, the selected references in chapter 6 will be useful if you want to pursue any of these topics further.

2 Watching Fishes

For some reason, watching birds as a pastime is not only acceptable but highly laudable; whereas anyone caught standing on a bridge ogling a stream through a pair of binoculars is automatically suspect. And the explanation that he's watching fish isn't going to help much. It simply never occurs to most people that it's possible to watch fish anywhere other than an aquarium. But it is, and I hope to entice you to get involved with these fascinating animals and become a fish watcher too.

Getting Started

You can start watching fishes in almost any body of water. Ponds in parks are usually a good bet, particularly if you see someone fishing there. Spring is the best time to start, but any warm month will do (more about that later). Begin by walking along the shore until you find a spot where the angle of the sun will let you see into the water. Once you can see the bottom or at least a few inches down into the water, you will be in business. Hold still and carefully look around the area where your view is clearest. Check any light patches of sand or pale rocks to see if there are fish over them, keeping in mind that some of the fishes may be very small, less than an inch long. Watch the surface of the water in smooth areas that are sheltered from the wind. If you see surface rings like those caused by raindrops but it isn't raining, you may be seeing evidence of small fishes feeding at the surface. Look for shadows on the bottom. If you see one that moves or is fish-shaped, you know there must be a fish somewhere between the shadow and the sun. Look for areas where the gravel seems to be cleaner than the surrounding bottom or where there is a shallow depression a foot or so in diameter. These may be sunfish nests. If they are, you should be able to find males guarding them.

In areas where the water is dark or the bottom is covered with dark particles, watch carefully to see if you can pick up flashes from the sides of small fishes as they dart about in pursuit of their prey or to escape their predators. Look carefully at any aquatic vegetation or any branches in the water. Many fishes spend most of the time hovering in such sheltered areas. Check the shadows of lily pads. Once you find fish, observe them long enough to see what they are doing. Are their fins moving? Is the mouth open or tightly closed? Are their gill covers moving? Are they facing into the current or downstream? Why is this fish here and not somewhere else? When you run out of questions (if you do), move on to another fish and see if you can think of more questions.

Park ponds are fine places to start, but you can expect some inter-ruptions from other park visitors, and of course you won't be able to wade in for a closer look. Sooner or later you are going to want to extend your fish watching to a wilder area with some creeks as well as standing water. I have always favored bridges because they en-able you to look directly down into the stream from a height. Gener-ally there are pools and perhaps riffles under the bridge that provide a variety of habitats. Also the bridge right of way is usually public property, so you don't have to be concerned about asking permis-sion to walk down to the stream bank.

Sometimes access to streams and private ponds can be a problem. The observer should always respect the rights of landowners and obtain permission before venturing onto private land. Most land-owners are quite reasonable if you ask first, but the same people can be justifiably very unpleasant if you trespass without permission. Fortunately, many streams are accessible to anglers and therefore to

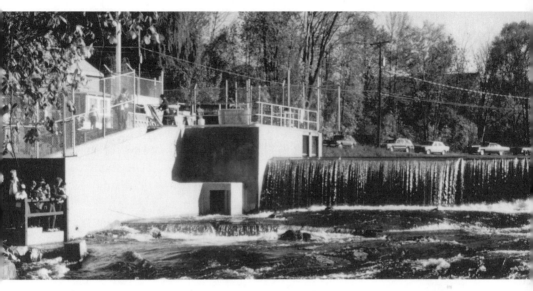

A fish ladder allows the fish to pass over falls and rapids and lets fish watchers observe the passage.

fish watchers as well. State lands are usually open to fishing, so you should have no problem there. Canals, either historic or active, are often excellent sites for fish watching. Wilderness lakes and rivers that are accessible only by canoe are ideal for watching all wildlife, terrestrial as well as aquatic.

For many observations you will want to wade out from shore. Go carefully, for your presence can disturb the bottom and damage fish nests. Be especially careful not to slide down a bank, lest you contribute to destruction of the shoreline. Streams and beaches can recover from mild disturbances as long as we all use common sense.

Once you find fish, what then? Your first question surely will be: What are they? Probably this will also be your most difficult question. Fish are seldom easy to identify, and as an observer looking down at a fish that evolution has protected from aerial attack, you are doubly disadvantaged. First, you see only the top of the fish, whereas all of the illustrations in guidebooks show the view from the side; and second, you are looking through water and usually from some distance. Here is where patience will pay off. Sooner or later the fish will roll on its side so that you can see some of its distinctive marks, such as the long "ear" flap of the redbreast sunfish or the vertical bars of the yellow perch. If you watch long enough, you will get a good idea of the true shape of the fish. With experience you will find behavior patterns and movements that provide clues to the identity of the fish, but of course you will have to be able to recognize the fish in order to get that experience. If you spend some time looking at pictures in books and visiting museums and aquariums whenever you get the chance, you will soon become familiar with most of the fishes of your area, and gradually you will acquire skill at identifying fish in the field.

Don't wait until you know what the fish is to record your observations, however. Give it a temporary descriptive name (numbers are usually harder to remember), whip out your notebook, and start your record as you get to work finding out just what those fish are up to.

Looking for Fishes

One of the major recreational uses of water is just looking at it. People enjoy ocean vistas, they are fascinated by waterfalls, and many select quiet lakeside resorts for their vacations. Riverbank restaurants are always popular and waterfront property fetches premium prices. Yet most people can stare at water for a long time without seeing any sign of life beneath the surface. The reason is that they haven't been told how to look for fish. If you know something about fishes and a little bit about how to look for them, you will soon find that you really can watch fishes and see what they are doing.

To begin with, one has to be aware that each body of water has its own special anatomy. When you first start to get interested in fishes, you may have to make a conscious effort to become aware of the particular features of the water environment. To a pheasant hunter a stream is just something that gets in the way; there is no reason to take special note of the stream itself. But to the fish watcher a quick inventory can reveal where one can look with a hope of seeing something, and may even suggest what one can expect to see. Learn to really study the water. In the beginning you may even want to make up a checklist that will help you remember what to look for, such as this one:

Aquatic Habitat Checklist

Streams
Width
Flow velocity
Bottom type
  Rock
  Boulders
  Cobbles
  Gravel
  Sand
  Mud
  Organic debris
Path
  Straight
  Meandering
  Braided (with multiple
    channels)
Profile
  Steep
  Gentle slope
  Barely perceptible slope
  Pools and riffles
  Falls and cascades
Shoreline
  Wooded
  Grassy
  Marshy
  Rocky
  Beaches
    Sandy
    Stony
Water
  Color
  Clarity

Particulate matter
Foam and froth
Valley
  U-shaped
  V-shaped
Alluvial terraces present or
  absent

Ponds and lakes
Size
Shape
Orientation
Water
  Color
  Clarity
Shoreline
  Contours
  Vegetation
    Wooded
    Grassland
    Urban
  Beaches
    Sand
    Shingle (stony)
  Bluffs
  Marshes
  Forested
  Rocky shores
  Gravel and cobbles
Obvious shoals and apparent
  deeps
Dams, gates, other artificial
  means to control water level
Inlets and outlets

After awhile this survey will become so automatic that you won't even realize you are making it when you look around and take in a general impression of the area.

Start with the surrounding land. Are there hills close by or is the country flat? Are the slopes gentle or steep? Steep hills suggest that the water may become quite deep a few yards offshore; flat marshy shores indicate extensive shoals close by. Is the area forested or is it covered with grasses? Are there tilled fields? What kind of fields? If the shores are pastureland, is there any indication that the pastures are in use? Sometimes the presence and arrangement of fences can tell a lot about how the land is being or has been used. The arrangement and extent of the shoreline, whether marsh or mudflat or soil bank or solid rock cliff, are important clues to the kinds of fishes you can expect to see in the water.

If the water is a stream, pay particular attention to its course. If it runs straight, look for signs that it has been artificially straightened. The presence of built-up banks or levees is an indication of human disturbance. Also note whether the banks have been protected by bulkheads (walls) or by linings of rocks (called riprap by engineers). Sometimes small check dams are built across streams to slow the runoff in times of flood. Look for the remains of old millraces or canal locks.

Next look at the stream itself. How fast is the water moving? Is the surface smooth or is it interrupted by a series of small waterfalls or riffles that divide the stream into separate pools? If aquatic plants are present, be sure to note where they grow and what kind they are. At first you can be content with general descriptions—water lilies, cattails, submerged aquatics, duckweed, whatever—but as you become more attuned to aquatic environments you will want to learn some of the aquatic plants too.

If you can see the bottom, note its color and type. Is it mud, sand, gravel, cobbles, boulders, or bedrock? Is it scoured clean or does it have a layer of silt or flocculent (fluffy) plant debris? If rocks are present, are they clean or covered with a layer of algae or by growths of plants and animals? Such growths are collectively called *Aufwuchs,* German for anything that grows on something else. In the spring some rocks in clear, cold streams may be covered with the larvae of blackflies.

The clarity and color of the water (gray, green, blue, or brown) are immediately apparent in a general way and can be measured more precisely with simple instruments. Of course you won't be able to see the chemical characteristics of the water—its acidity, dissolved oxygen content, or whether it is polluted with sewage, fertilizers, or persistent pesticides—but in time you will learn to make a good guess at even these characteristics. A thermometer and a vial of pH papers from the aquarium store will give you a start.

Streams that cascade and tumble over rocks are very pretty and good for the trout fisher, but the greatest variety of fishes will be found in more sedate streams that provide a greater variety of habitats—pools and riffles, undercut banks and meanders, sandbars and backwaters with a fallen tree or a clump of weeds here and there. Ultimately the number of species present is determined by the number of available microhabitats.

In order to see the fishes we must have flat water or some means of looking through the surface disturbance caused by wind and water movement. Most streams have some sheltered areas where the water is calm enough to see through. There may be small patches of calm water downstream of rocks and logs or in the lee of banks and boulders. Shifting currents and swirls cause temporary flat areas that permit a quick glimpse below the surface. The experienced fish watcher learns to take advantage of these temporary windows in the surface.

The trick to seeing into the water is to avoid surface glare. Polaroid sunglasses help, but even under the best of conditions you have to find a direction where the reflection from the sky does not interfere with your viewing. Clear, sunny days are better for seeing into the water than overcast days, and you can usually see better when the sun is high in the sky than in the late afternoon or early morning, when it is low on the horizon.

Another way to get around the surface glare is to use a glass-bottom bucket or "water telescope." The problem with using a glass-bottom bucket in shallow water is that you have to get so close to the fish that you scare them away. You'll find this device more useful when you work deeper waters from a boat.

Some of the best viewing is from high above the water. Bridges, overhanging trees, piers and high bulkheads, and high banks are good places to start looking. In fact, a committed fish watcher always heads for a high vantage point first, to see what fish are visible. This is where your binoculars can be used to good advantage.

Even under the best conditions you have to be willing to work to see fish. Start with the assumption that the fish are there and that it's simply a matter of finding them. Remember that if the fish were easy to see, their predators could see them too. Most fish are countershaded—that is, they are dark on top and lighter underneath. This arrangement balances out the light that is reflected from them: the dark upper surface absorbs the direct light while the pale underside reflects light and cancels out the shadows. As long as the fish remains motionless, it is very hard to detect. In shallow water we can often see its shadow on the bottom much more easily than we can see the fish itself. When the water is very muddy, fish swimming near the surface sometimes appear as clear holes in the milky brown water.

Some fishes have conspicuous marks that seem likely to give them away but in fact have the opposite effect. The marks break up the outline of the fish and thus make it more difficult for us, and probably for their natural predators, to recognize them as fish.

Fish are usually easier to detect when they are moving. Often you can stare into a pool for a long time without seeing much of anything until a fish turns on its side and its silvery scales reflect the sunlight. This may even be the first sign of a sizable school of fish, hidden by their camouflage but betrayed by the movement of one of their members. Fish swimming near the surface sometimes produce a visible wake, and actively feeding or spawning fish may roll or jump clear of the surface. Relatively few fish, however, spend any appreciable amount of time at the surface; most are midwater or bottom dwellers. An exception is the needlefish, which lives at the surface in the brackish parts of estuaries and occasionally moves upstream to fresh water. Other surface dwellers are some killifishes and the freshwater silverside *Labidesthes sicculus*. Gars and sturgeons some-times bask at the surface.

Sometimes a fish swimming below the surface produces a wake that reaches the surface some distance behind it. These wakes then look as if they were caused by a fish that was larger—sometimes much larger—than it really is. Here may lie the source of local mon-ster legends.

Fish are most fun to watch, of course, when they are active. When they are feeding on insects at the surface they make swirls, and often their momentum carries them clear of the surface. Late eve-nings and early mornings are peak feeding times for many species. Certain sunfishes make an audible pop as they feed at the surface, and a careful observer may be able to recognize the species by their feeding sounds.

Many fish tend to move into shallow water at night. If you prowl the shoreline with a flashlight, you may see species that tend to keep to deep water during the day. Often these fish "freeze" when the light hits them and allow you to get a good look at them. Be careful, though: some species develop night color patterns that make them look quite different from the way they look in daylight.

The sunfish family, which includes the largemouth and small-mouth basses, contains some of the most interesting species to watch. Nearly all sunfishes build nests in shallow water, sometimes where the water is only a few inches deep. They are frequently seen in park ponds, oblivious of people strolling by only a few feet away. You can make yourself comfortable and watch the whole process. Here we see another advantage of fish watching. You can be the judge of how much you want to put into it. You haven't paid for a ticket and you don't have to stay any longer than you really want to. You can just glance at the nest and say "Isn't that nice," or you can concentrate on seeing all that is going on. You can watch the male building the nest, courting the females, the spawning act, and the guarding of the nest and care of the young. You can take notes on what species the male chases, how many females he courts and their responses, and how many courtship attempts end in actual spawn-ing. You can come back the next day to see when the spawning starts, how long it continues, and what effect the weather has on the spawning process. You can watch the rest of the week or the rest of the month. But you don't have to.

Beachcombing is another favorite activity of the dedicated fish watcher. Some fish species are seldom seen except as dead carcasses washed up on a beach. Dead fish are not always aesthetically pleasing, but as scavengers clean the skeletons they become more tolerable. Many fish bones are so beautiful that some sculptors use them as models or for inspiration. Fishes can be identified from their skeletons, frequently from single diagnostic bones. The serious fish watcher may want to assemble a collection of fish bones with which unidentified specimens can be compared. When you find skeletons that are quite clean but still held together by ligaments, you can appreciate the intricate mechanical operation of the skeleton.

Keep in mind that the fishes' notion of a desirable environment may not correspond with our aesthetic concepts. Some species delight in areas that seem distinctly unsavory to the fish watcher's eye. It is not for us to judge where the fish should be; our task is to find out where they are. Sometimes our search will take us to sparkling mountain brooks but at other times we may find ourselves downwind of a sewer outfall. In the process we are sure to learn more about aquatic environments, and about our own environment as well.

Equipment

Naturalists' most important tools are their notebooks. Careful records of observations kept for a period of time soon begin to reveal patterns, and a study of these patterns is one of the best ways to learn about almost any subject. Notebooks need not be fancy, but it's a good idea to choose a readily available type and stick to it so that they are easy to file and keep organized. Most field notebooks get kind of messy, but never mind—the wear and tear are good evidence that the notes were made in the field, not written from memory in comfort at the end of the day. If you have a personal computer, you might try storing your field notes in a file. Some of the better word processing programs make it possible to sort records and even index your notes for ready accessibility.

Other than your notebook, you need no special equipment to watch fish. Polaroid glasses help cut glare from the water's surface and binoculars are useful, particularly when it is possible to observe from a high vantage point such as a bridge or a tree limb. A camera with a telephoto lens and a polarizing filter will sometimes record fishes that are barely visible to the unaided eye. For wading or observing from a boat, a simple glass-bottom bucket will be very useful.

In flat country even as simple a thing as following a stream course can be difficult. I find that good maps, preferably the topographic maps prepared by the U.S. Geological Survey, are almost indispensable.

Sometimes you will want to do some observing in the water. If you don't mind getting wet, you can use a face mask and snorkel or, for the trained driver, scuba (self-contained underwater breathing apparatus). Scuba divers often feel that if they are going to dive, they want to go as deep as they can; the idea of lying on the bottom in water they could stand in is not attractive. The problem with this thinking is that the fish are often carrying out their activities in quite shallow water. Scuba gear permits you to lie on the bottom where you can really see what is going on, and you can remain still long enough to permit the fish to get used to you and return to nearly normal activity patterns. So even in very shallow water scuba is preferable to a snorkel, which requires you to return to the surface to breathe after a few seconds on the bottom. Even if you are not diving, you will often find yourself in the water, wading out to get a good look at a nest or working your way around a cliff or a fallen tree. In warm weather a bathing suit and a pair of old sneakers to protect your feet are all you really need, but sometimes more protection is called for. Stream banks are favorite haunts of stinging nettles, poison ivy, and various spine-bearing grasses, vines, and trees. In some environments there are leeches and, even worse, an affliction familiarly known as swimmer's itch, which is caused by cercaria, larvae of a small worm that are shed by certain snails and burrow into the skin. Flies and other insects can be troublesome at times.

You can avoid most of these minor problems by wearing expendable clothes over your bathing suit. A diver's wet suit may be preferred by those with a flair for the dramatic. It is also nice to have a set of dry clothes to change into at the end of the day's outing. In deep or swift water a flotation device such as a working life jacket is a good safety precaution.

In cold weather getting wet is not so pleasant. You should consider hip boots, or better, chest-high waders of the type used by trout fishers. You can make them more slipproof by gluing pieces of outdoor carpeting or felt to the soles with contact cement. In a fast-moving stream or near deep water, losing one's balance can be more than uncomfortable. Air trapped in waders can make swimming difficult or impossible. Never wear waders in a boat.

Sometimes you may want to catch a specimen or two to check their identification. You can try a minnow trap or a seine or dip net as well as regular fishing gear. Be sure to check the local and state game laws to find out which gear and fishing methods are permitted. Some states allow the use of small nets for collecting bait, and these nets are ideal for catching specimens to examine and identify. You will almost surely need a fishing license, and for some kinds of collecting a special scientific collector's permit may be necessary. These permits are usually issued only to recognized scientists and teachers, so most fish watchers will be limited to species that are not protected by conservation laws. Fortunately, these species include many of the most interesting ones. Clear glass or plastic jars will allow you to study small fish and then return them to the water from which they came. Always remember not to touch the fish without wetting your hands first; otherwise you will remove some of the protective slime, which is their first defense against infection by bacteria and other pathogens.

Other items that may prove useful to the dedicated fish watcher are a stopwatch for timing flow rates and activity patterns, a thermometer for taking air and water temperature, a vial of pH papers, a secchi disk to measure water clarity, a small quantity of 70 percent alcohol for preserving insects and other specimens, a hiker's staff to help you cross streams, the kind of emergency supplies used by hikers, and perhaps a small tape recorder for taking notes. Such things can be added as you discover a need for them. For now, start simply and don't forget your lunch.

A fish-watching enthusiast with all the money in the world could invest in advanced rebreather diving gear, which recirculates the inert gases in the air the diver breathes and replaces only the oxygen that is actually used. With one of these outfits a diver can remain in the water for twelve hours or more at a time. Underwater "habitats" allow divers to remain underwater for weeks on end, and submersible vehicles can reach the deepest parts of the ocean. Recently underwater technology has centered on ROVs (remotely operated vehicles), which are self-propelled devices equipped with television cameras and manipulator arms controlled from the surface. You send the ROV down and "fly" it around while watching the underwater world on a television screen. You can control the mechanical arm from the surface, too, if you want to collect samples or repair a power cable.

These wonderful tools have opened up new ways of studying and working in the deep waters of the world. But so far they're not for the average fish watcher. Apart from the cost and technical personnel needed, they don't help much in turbid waters, and that is the biggest problem for the shoreside fish watcher. Maybe someday electronic detectors will produce clear images in full color, but then we would be seeing the fish on television and not in the wild.

Taking Notes

One key to enjoying any kind of natural history is to keep notes on your observations and refer to them frequently. Fish are exciting to watch, and in a sense watching them is its own reward. After a few months, however, memories begin to fade and past events start to run together. But with a good record of your outings, you can relive the most exciting parts of your fish-watching career.

Record your observations as you make them, not a week or even a day later. It is important to transcribe and supplement the record while it is still fresh in your mind. Some observers find that a consistent format—perhaps even a preprinted form—for recording standard data such as date, time, location, weather, and habitat description ensures that none of the essential facts are missed. A small tape recorder, suitably protected from the weather, will let you take notes without taking your eyes off the action. Dictate your notes as if you were telling the story to your best (and most patient) friend.

Every once in awhile review your notes to see what patterns are emerging. If you see suckers spawning on June 5, check back to see when you saw them spawning last year and the year before. The timing of such events is one of the most interesting aspects of natural history. Such phenomena as the blooming of wildflowers are triggered largely by length of daylight and occur almost on the same day each year. Other events are more dependent on temperature and may occur earlier in warm years than in cool years. Degree-day figures, published in the weather sections of some newspapers, provide a useful basis for comparison.

Don't be afraid of a little arithmetic. If you see a school of suckers in a pool, try to estimate how many are in the school. Try the old cowboy trick of counting a group of ten or so and then estimating how many such groups make up the school. Crude as such estimates are, they give you an idea of the number of fish in the pool, and if you repeat the estimates over a few days, you may find out whether the school is increasing, decreasing, or remaining constant. Another good basis for comparing habitats is the use of ratios, such as the relative numbers of sunfish and smallmouth bass. This estimate doesn't demand an exact count but it provides a lot of information about the fishes and their environmental requirements. If one area has twenty sunfish for every bass and another has five, you can start to wonder what causes the difference.[1]

1. There could be many reasons why the first area is better suited to sunfishes than to bass. Perhaps it provides more shelter for the smaller sunfishes; or more people catch bass there; or it has higher temperatures that favor sunfish; or the bass in the second area feed heavily on sunfishes; or the water in the first area is too shallow for bass; or any number of other things. If you watch carefully, perhaps you can find out.

Many people are reluctant to attempt such counts because they know the counts are not exact. This is a universal problem and it is the reason why professional fisheries scientists, whose counts are only slightly more precise than yours, make use of elaborate statistical procedures to work with data that are less than perfect. Even if you are not interested in the statistical side, try a few simple graphs to help you see important patterns. For example, if you are camped on a lake and see fish rising in late afternoon, count the number of surface swirls in a period of perhaps two minutes. Repeat the count at half-hour intervals until it gets too dark to see. Plot these counts against time and see what the line looks like. Does the number of swirls increase as the sun goes down? Does the frequency of feeding increase steadily or is there a sudden flurry of activity that ends as abruptly as it began? Does the frequency rise to a peak and then decline before the sun sets, or is it still rising when it becomes too dark to make any more counts?

Photographers will want to supplement their notes with pictures of the area, of fish nests, and possibly such activities as spawning. Videotapes are especially good for recording activities, for when you replay them you can often see things you failed to notice at the time.

For identification, good lateral views are preferable to shots that may be more "artistic" but that make it difficult to interpret proportions, locations of distinguishing marks, and so forth. A setup for taking pictures in the field consists of a narrow aquarium with a nonglare glass front and a glass plate that can be used to crowd the fish against the front glass. For the background, a shallow box with a frosted glass front can be placed behind the aquarium to provide uniform illumination. The inside of the box is painted white and the light that enters is reflected in such a way that it eliminates hot spots. A plastic ruler can be positioned to provide scale and a color swatch can be added as a check on the fidelity of the colors in the photograph.

For even greater control, serious photographers devise a system of strobe lights positioned so as to eliminate reflections and shadows.

Setup for field photography.

Fish Watching by the Calendar

There is nothing subtle about the seasons in the temperate zone. The tropics are all right, I suppose, but I pity people who live where the weather is always warm to hot and winter is indistinguishable from summer. Seasons always come as a shock to me. Intellectually I know they are inevitable, but emotionally they always catch me by surprise. There is no denying that some times of the year are better for watching fishes than others, but no season should be totally excluded.

Winter

Winter is not a particularly good time for watching fishes but it is an excellent time to explore their habitats and generally to get ready for spring. With the leaves off the trees one can see stream courses and the shorelines of lakes and ponds. When the ice gets thick enough, you can walk across ponds and along lakeshores to explore coves and marshes that can't even be seen in the summer. When the aquatic vegetation dies back, the whole appearance of the shallows changes.

Ice fishing is a popular sport, and many lakes suddenly become small cites of ice fishers' shanties. Get acquainted with some ice fishers or try it yourself. Find out what they are catching and how. Bait and tackle shops are good places to start. In some areas ice fishers have interesting tricks, such as using bright-colored decoys to lure pike and other fish within range of their spears. When the ice is clear, spend some time looking to see if any fish are visible. Look carefully, because they won't be very active. Check out the icefree sections near falls and rapids to see if any fish are visible.

Most fish are pretty sluggish in cold water and they don't feed or grow very much. Some are active all winter long, though, and these, of course, are the species that come to the angler's bait. Yellow perch and northern pike are pretty active throughout the winter. Rainbow trout spawn from December to April in the Great Lakes region and tomcod enter the coastal estuaries from the Hudson River northward to spawn in January.

A fascinating thing happens under some winter conditions. If circumstances are just right—if there is no snow cover to insulate the ground, the temperature dips very low, and rocks stick out of the water to act as cooling fins—the water temperature can drop rapidly to below the freezing point while it continues to flow. At such times small ice crystals form and stick to any objects in the water. Flocculent ice accumulates on rocks and gravel so that in an hour or two the stream can become choked with a thick layer of "anchor ice." As the ice forms, it displaces the water and the stream rises, sometimes overflowing its banks. When the sun comes up, the ice melts as quickly as it formed, and soon the only evidence of the anchor ice is a line of surface ice attached to the bank well above normal water level. Sometimes the ice melts so quickly that fish are left stranded. Anchor ice can harm trout nests by lifting the gravel to which it is attached and exposing the developing eggs or young trout.

Winter is a good time to visit a trout hatchery. Since brook and

In the off season visit fish hatcheries and aquariums.

brown trout spawn in the late fall and rainbows spawn in early spring, cold-water hatcheries usually have eggs developing during the winter. Most hatcheries operated on public money have displays and exhibits explaining their operations. Salmon hatcheries such as the one on a Lake Ontario tributary at Altmar, New York, are especially interesting.

Winter is also a good time to visit aquariums and to snuggle up with a good fish book.

Spring

Spring is by far the most exciting time of year for the fish watcher. The majority of our fishes spawn when temperatures are rising and day length is increasing. Even as the ice leaves, and sometimes before it does, pikes and pickerels move into shallows to spawn. Spring is the season when many of the minnows and darters put on their brightest colors as they move into riffles to establish their territories and try to attract mates. As the season progresses, sunfish nests appear in the shallows. Largemouth and smallmouth bass spawn early in the spring. They are followed by pumpkinseeds and bluegills, whose nesting activities continue well into the summer months.

March, April, and May are the months of the sucker runs. Suckers move into small streams to spawn over gravel riffles. Sometimes small pools have large numbers of suckers a foot or two long resting between spawning episodes. Spawning is easily observed. Groups consisting of one female accompanied by several males swim upstream together with their bodies pushed into the gravel and their dorsal fins and tails awash, lashing the water into a furious wake.

March is also a good time to see the walleye run at the state fish hatchery at Constantia, New York, on Oneida Lake. The sight is worth the trip. But wherever you are in early spring, get out and walk along the nearest beach. Fish that have died over the winter begin to float to the surface and wash up on shore, where we can get a good look at them.

Summer

During the summer months things sort of taper off. Except for a few sunfishes and bullheads starting second families, the spawning season is over. If you wear shorts, watch out for nettles along the stream courses. Weeds are high in the fields and the sounds of farm machinery echo across the valleys. Most of the fishes have established a summer routine, just as we land animals have done.

Still, it's a good time for fish watching. The water levels are low and the streams are warm and clear. Get out your notebook and see what you can learn about habitat preference. See where the minnow schools are, watch the darters resting on the bottom, and watch a skilled fly fisher work her favorite stream. See the stonerollers and suckers as they vacuum-clean the pebbles and stone slabs on the bottom. Take lots of notes and review them to see if any observations that didn't mean much at the time begin to show a pattern. Sit under a tree and chew a timothy stem as you think about what you have been seeing.

For the fishes this is a time of promise. Tiny sunfish fry have left their nests and now lurk among the rocks and vegetation, hidden by a pattern of bold vertical bars across their transparent bodies. Clouds of black bullhead fry patrol the shores together but soon they will go their separate ways. Smallmouth fry with tricolor tails skulk among the rocks in seeming defiance of their predators. Schools of quillback suckers and gizzard shads loaf in the quiet lower reaches of larger creeks.

Food is plentiful and the waters are warm. The mission of young fishes now is to eat as much food as they can and turn it into solid flesh before the temperature drops and prey becomes scarce.

Don't forget that the fish have their active times and their quiet times. Try prowling the shore as the sun goes down and early in the morning before the air warms up. Fire up the Coleman lantern and row along the shore after dark. You will probably find that the night shift consists of a different group of fishes as the diurnal species retire and the nocturnal forms come out for their turn.

Summer is the time to get out the mask and snorkel and join the fish. Dive down and look under rocks and in caves. Float with the current in streams. Cool off and enjoy your fish watching.

Fall

In the fall the trout and salmon spawn. This is the season when you will see the shores of the Great Lakes lined with anglers casting their snag hooks in the hope of connecting with a coho or king salmon. When they do, the rewards are well worth the effort, for these introduced Pacific salmons often weigh 20 pounds or more. Even if you don't fish yourself, you should take advantage of the opportunity to see these species that otherwise spend their lives in the deeps of large lakes where they cannot be seen. Brook and brown trout spawn in smaller streams; ciscos and whitefishes spawn in lakes, where their spawning rituals sometimes bring them to the surface so that the boating observer can at least see that something is going on, even if the details are lost.

As the days get shorter and the water cools, the fish feed less and less until their growth all but stops. The fish become less active and move into deeper and quieter water, where they conserve their energy and wait for spring. The fish watcher heads for the bookstore.

3   *Fish Watching by Habitat*

This chapter is intended to be used in the field. The material is arranged by habitat type. The Key to Fish Habitats will help you decide which section to consult. In each section you will find a brief discussion of the special features of the habitat and the families of fishes that you can expect to see there. Keep in mind, however, that fish select microhabitats, not overall habitat type. Where you see a pond the fish sees a patch of weeds.

The habitat categories used here are probably unique. Most working stream biologists use some more complex system based on gradient, bottom type, flow rate, temperature, water quality, stream order, and the like. My system may be less precise but it is based on features that will be obvious as soon as you reach the shore.

Some species are limited to a single habitat, but most species live in several. The brook trout is found in rocky headwater creeks, in cool swampy creeks, and also in ponds. The smallmouth bass and some other sunfishes inhabit streams as well as lakes. Channel catfishes live in large streams and lakes. Still, the habitat is the logical starting point because this is what we land animals see first.

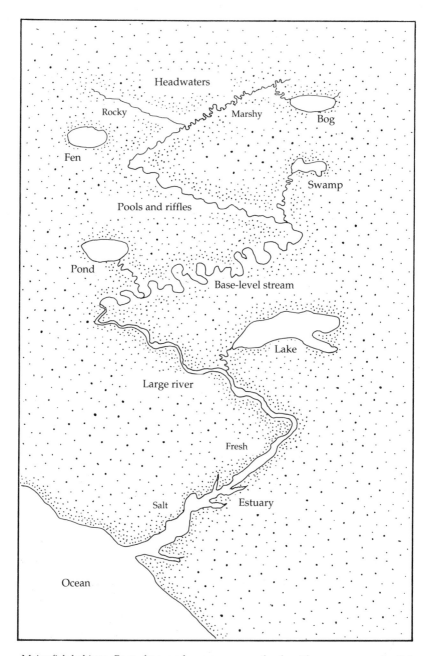

Major fish habitats. Bogs, fens, and swamps are wetlands with some open-water fish habitats. Headwaters are arbitrarily designated as rocky or marshy. An estuary can have a freshwater tidal portion as well as a saltwater section. Habitat types are rarely arranged as neatly as they are here. Sections of pool-and-riffle habitat, for example, may alternate with meandering base-level habitat as the slope and underlying geological features change.

Key to Fish Habitats

Flowing waters

Small streams originating in springs or wetlands, generally with an average width of less than 10 feet . . . . Headwater streams

    Rocky-bottom streams in V-shaped valleys . . . . Rocky creeks

    Slow meandering streams with swampy or marshy banks . . . . Marshy creeks

Larger streams, generally more than 10 feet wide

    "Natural" streams; that is, streams not used for navigation

        Streams with conspicuous pools and riffles . . . . Mid-reach streams

        Sluggish, meandering streams; may have occasional sandbars but few or no conspicuous pools and riffles . . . . Base-level streams

    Large rivers used for navigation

        Fresh water . . . . Large rivers

        Flowing into oceans; lower reaches brackish or salt water . . . . Estuaries

Standing waters (may have inlet and outlet streams)

Permanent, standing water with heavy vegetation and little or no open water . . . . Wetlands

Permanent standing water with rock or completely vegetated shoreline . . . . Ponds and small lakes

Permanent standing water with at least some rocky or sandy, wave-swept shoreline . . . . Large lakes

Flowing Waters

Any boat owner can tell you that water is a mobile fluid, always on the go and going pretty much where it wants to, regardless of any efforts to contain or exclude it.

Fresh water ultimately starts as rain. Some rainwater evaporates almost as soon as it lands, some is absorbed by plants and animals, some flows over the land surface directly into streams, and some soaks into the ground, where it makes it way through soils and rocks into the groundwater system. Many permanent streams are fed by springs—that is, groundwater—as well as by runoff.

Stream fish are controlled by many factors. Particularly important is the size of the stream, the velocity of the water, and its quality. Streams can be classified in a variety of ways, but for our purposes it is useful to characterize them as headwater, mid-reach, and base-level streams. Headwater streams are those in which most erosion occurs upstream and little sediment is deposited. Mid-reach streams are those that erode both the banks and the bottom as pools alternate with riffles. Base-level streams have low gradients so that most erosion is lateral and considerable deposition of sediments causes the stream to meander.

Topography and the underlying geological framework can give a stream several cycles of mid-reach and base-level sections. Therefore, it is not unusual to find a base-level stretch upstream from a mid-reach section.

Base-level streams grade into large rivers, which I think of as those streams that are used for navigation and the industry that goes with the availability of water transportation.

Then there are estuaries, water passages where rivers flow into the sea. Salt water pushes up under the fresh water as the river meets the sea, and the water becomes increasingly saline toward the coast. Because estuaries are at sea level, they are affected by tides.

Headwater Streams: Rocky Creeks

CHARACTERISTICS. Rocky headwater streams range from the tiny brooks that mark the recognizable beginnings of streams to rather sizable, almost torrential creeks. They flow directly from runoff and upland springs and the smaller brooks may be intermittent—that is, flowing only during the wetter parts of the year and drying completely in late summer. Usually rocky headwaters have steep gradients in V-shaped valleys and have nearly straight courses. Even the larger rocky streams, say those with an average width of more than 25 feet, have boulder and rock or gravel bottoms with relentless swift currents and few pools where the water is relatively quiet. They usually have little visible vegetation.

Steep profile

Few or no pools

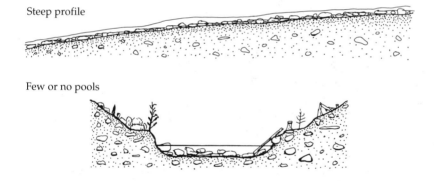

Nearly straight course

Profile, cross section, and plan of a rocky headwater stream. The stream bed is filled with rocks and there are few or no pools.

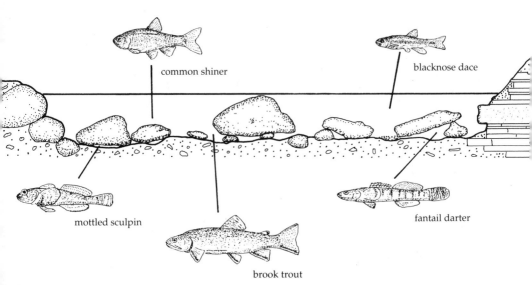

Habitat selection in a rocky headwater stream. Common shiners and blacknose dace frequent the open waters while the mottled sculpin, brook trout, and fantail darter keep to shelter under and near rocks.

MICROHABITATS. Rocky creeks do not have a lot of variety but there will be fast-water flumes where the water is channeled by boulders and rock outcrops, interspersed with protected areas of quiet water around larger boulders. There may be falls with pools at the bottom and crevices between layers of rocks. Undercut banks and fallen trees and logs provide a different type of shelter. Sandbars sometimes build up at the mouths of tributaries.

WHAT TO LOOK FOR IN ROCKY CREEKS. Relatively few species live in the smaller headwater streams. Those streams that dry in the summer will of course have no permanent residents, but some fish may move in when water is running. Blacknose dace are often found in such situations. Sometimes brook trout spawn in small streams and the young remain there as long as the water is flowing. Farther down, where the water flows year round, more species are to be expected, and you may find creek chubs, lake chubs, cutlips minnows, longnose dace, pearl dace, sculpins, johnny darters, and fantail darters, to name only a few.

Fishes are hard to see in fast-flowing water, so look in the still places where rocks break the flow.

The longnose dace, *Rhinichthys cataractae,* is a fish of moving waters.

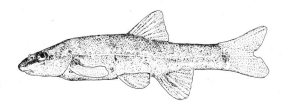

The blacknose dace, *Rhinichthys atratulus.*

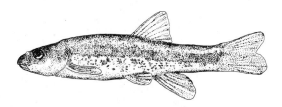

The barred fantail darter, *Etheostoma flabellare.*

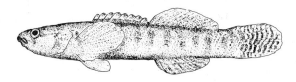

The mottled sculpin, *Cottus bairdi.*

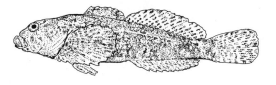

Headwater Streams: Marshy Creeks

CHARACTERISTICS. Marshy headwater streams drain low-lying areas that are fed by springs. Some are slow, tortuously meandering brooks linked with alders; others flow through grassy marshes. Sometimes they are dammed by beavers. Often the water is stained dark brown and much of the bottom is covered with flocculent organic debris from vegetation in the stream and along the shore. Submerged aquatic vegetation may form dense beds.

MICROHABITATS. Marshy creeks are somewhat more diverse than rocky creeks. The bottom may be clay, mud, or organic debris. Much of the shoreline consists of peat or roots of swamp plants. Floods may wash in a log here and there. Meandering streams often have

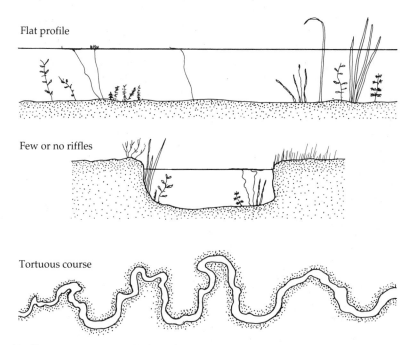

Flat profile

Few or no riffles

Tortuous course

Profile, cross section, and plan of a marshy headwater stream. The slow-moving water and tortuous channel allow growth of varied and sometimes dense aquatic vegetation.

This aerial view shows the meanders of a marshy headwater stream. Parts of it may have been straightened artificially.

undercut banks on the outsides of the curves and sandbars on the inner sides. Patches of vegetation provide shelter for small fishes.

WHAT TO LOOK FOR IN MARSHY CREEKS. Marshy creeks have more microhabitats and therefore larger faunas than rocky headwater streams. Their banks are often formed of the peaty remains of plants and by the roots of living plants. The streams may be shaded by alders or grasses that hang out over the water. As a result of this shading, along with their underground source, headwaters tend to be cool, rather stable environments. In northern streams we may find the familiar blacknose dace–brook trout community and we may also find such species as redside dace, finescale dace, creek chubs, lake chubs, pearl dace, bridled shiners, common shiners, johnny darters, pirate perch, white suckers, possibly brook stick-lebacks, killifishes, and mudminnows. In the south we will find no

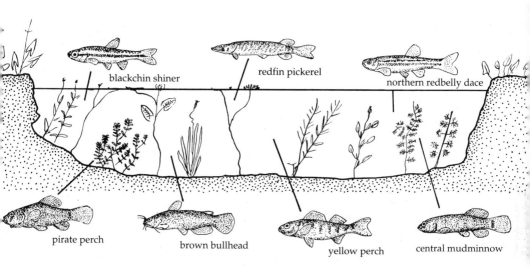

Habitat selection in a marshy headwater stream. The blackchin shiner, redfin pickerel, and redbelly dace spend most of their time near the surface in clear weedy waters. The pirate perch lives in dense vegetation and the mudminnow near the bottom among plant debris. The larger brown bullhead keeps to the bottom while the yellow perch hovers higher up in the water column.

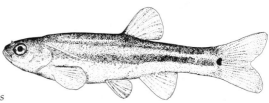

The northern redbelly dace, *Phoxinus eos*.

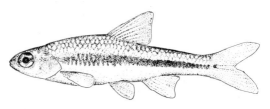

The blackchin shiner, *Notropis heterodon*.

trout, but look for pirate perch, killifishes, livebearers, and an array of darters and minnows.

The water in marshy creeks characteristically is stained a dark brown, so fishes may be hard to see in the shadows and when they are under the roots of shore vegetation. Look for larger pools in clearings, and in areas where the water is bubbling up from springs you may find pale bottoms. Watch these spots to see if you can see fish as they swim over the lighter background. On bright days you may be able to see fish shadows even when the bottom is covered with dark-brown or gray organic sediments.

Marshy creeks can also flow directly into swampy or marshy shorelines of lakes and ponds, and their lower reaches may be home to species of sunfishes and perches that we normally expect to find in lakes or ponds.

Mid-Reach Streams: Pools and Riffles

CHARACTERISTICS. Mid-reach stream have alternating pools and riffles, a riffle being a section of the stream where current is deflected as it flows over rock or gravel so that the surface is permanently disturbed. Mid-reach streams range from a few feet to many yards across. They also vary in gradient (steepness) and in bottom type.

MICROHABITATS. As we proceed downstream, the land slopes less steeply and the gradient of the stream decreases. The alternating riffles and pools provide more microhabitats where fishes can find their preferred conditions. As mid-reach streams are larger than headwater streams, they provide varied shelter. Sand and gravel bars develop on the insides of the curves, and the banks on the outsides of the curves are often undercut. Aquatic plants are abundant and varied. Some parts of the streams are shaded by overhanging branches and other sections are relatively exposed. Here and there erosion causes trees to fall into the stream, and deep pools tend to form around their roots. In streams that are subject to flood-

Stepped profile

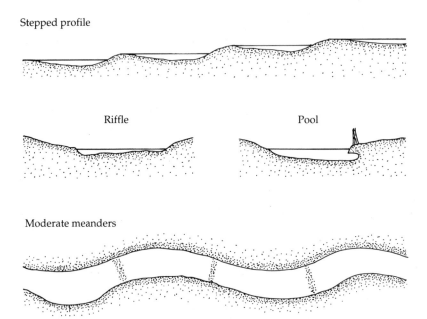

Riffle

Pool

Moderate meanders

Profile, cross section, and plan of a pool-and-riffle stream. The riffles are caused by the flow of rapid water over sand, gravel, or rocky shallows. Pools often have sandbars on one side and undercut banks on the other.

ing, some pools are nearly or completely cut off from the main stream. With heavy rains these pools come and go as the sand and gravel bars shift. Such semipermanent pools are good places to see fish because they are free of currents and often quite clear, and the fish either are trapped here or can exit only by a narrow passage, which they try to avoid unless they are seriously disturbed. In keeping with the greater variety of habitats, more kinds of fish are present here than in headwater streams.

Waterfalls are common in mid-reach streams. Big waterfalls, such as Niagara, are overwhelming, and high falls with their spectacular downstream gorges can hold our attention for hours as we watch the ever-changing pattern of the falling water. Even low falls and cascades over rocky outcrops and artificial cataracts over dams are fascinating. For some reason no one knows, rapidly flowing water casts a special spell on the human psyche.

Falls and rapids are good for fish, too. The violently stirred water rapidly comes into equilibrium with the atmosphere, absorbing all the oxygen it can hold and getting rid of undesirable gases such as carbon dioxide and methane. Even pollutants such as PCBs are released, and show up in higher concentrations in plants and animals living around waterfalls. Fishes that require high levels of oxygen tend to thrive in fast-flowing waters and downstream from waterfalls.

WHAT TO LOOK FOR IN MID-REACH STREAMS. The fishes that live in pool-and-riffle streams often are very selective in their choice of habitats. Some are definitely pool dwellers, others are distinctly more at home in riffles. Don't expect this to be an absolute rule, though. Some fish spend, say, 80 percent of their time in riffles and 20 percent in pools, and others spend 90 percent in pools and 10 percent in riffles.

In the pools look for minnows such as the common shiner and the silver shiner, and for perch, sunfishes, and smallmouth bass with their tricolor tails. In cooler streams watch for trout lurking under

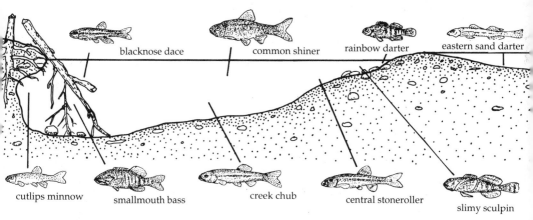

blacknose dace   common shiner   rainbow darter   eastern sand darter

cutlips minnow   smallmouth bass   creek chub   central stoneroller   slimy sculpin

Habitat selection in a pool-and-riffle stream. The oblique section reveals an undercut bank at the left and a shallow riffle at the right. A cutlips minnow and a smallmouth bass lurk in the shelter of the bank and among the branches of a fallen tree. Common shiners inhabit more open water and creek chubs stay near the bottom of pools. Stoneroller minnows select the foot of a riffle, while sculpins and the rainbow darter live amid the gravel of the shallows. Just above the riffle an eastern sand darter lives in fine sand that is kept clean by the water as it picks up speed before flowing over the riffle.

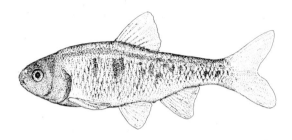

The breeding male common shiner, *Luxilus cornutus*.

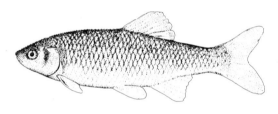

The rosyface shiner, *Notropis rubellus*.

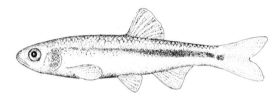

The spotfin shiner, *Cyprinella spiloptera*.

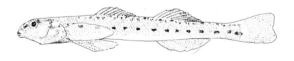

The eastern sand darter, *Ammocrypta pellucida*.

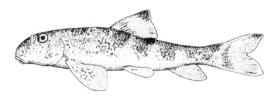

The northern hog sucker, *Hypentelium nigricans*.

logs and undercut banks. Small white suckers are nearly ubiquitous in mid-reach streams.

It is harder to see fish in the riffles, but this is where you will find darters, madtom catfishes, sculpins, and in the lower parts of the riffles and in nearby pools stoneroller minnows. Interestingly enough, the longnose dace is a riffle species in streams but it also lives along the windswept shores of large lakes. Apparently both of these seemingly different environments supply the moving water and cobble rock shelters that the species needs. Other species that live in both lakes and streams usually prefer the areas where water movement is minimal.

Base-Level Streams

CHARACTERISTICS. Base-level streams are slow-moving, usually meandering streams with few riffles. They frequently have sandbars on the insides of the curves and undercut banks on the outsides. Often the water is muddy or deeply stained. They tend to be larger than mid-reach streams and subject to periodic flooding. These are the streams that southerners call bayous.

MICROHABITATS. Low-gradient streams are often quite uniform mile after mile. Only the depth, vegetation, and bottom type vary as the stream winds its way through meadows, farms, and occasional patches of forest. Sandbars and weed beds provide excellent fish habitat. In flat country that is subject to periodic flooding, a sandy-

Very low gradient

Occasional sand
and gravel shallows

Flume   Shallows

Deep meanders

Profile, cross section, and plan of a base-level stream. Shallow sand and gravel or rocky outcrops produce occasional riffles in such a low-gradient, sluggish stream with deep meanders, but most of the stream is relatively deep and flumelike. Sediments are deposited on the insides of the curves; the banks on the outsides of the curves may be undercut by the current.

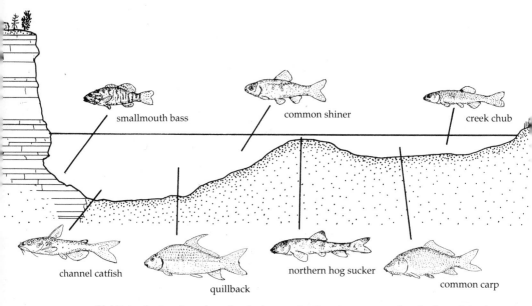

Habitat selection in a base-level stream. As the stream meanders back and forth across the valley, it frequently cuts into higher ground to form steep cliffs. Rocks and overhangs at the base of a cliff provide good shelter for catfish and smallmouth bass. Quillback suckers and common shiners share the pools, and hog suckers are seen in the shallows. Common carp and creek chubs also tend to stay in shallow areas.

bottom stream may have multiple channels so that it appears to consist of interwoven strands of water. Such streams are called, appropriately enough, braided streams. Base-level streams usually have many logs and fallen trees that provide excellent shelter for fishes. Often you will find places where the banks are deeply undercut and the soil has eroded away from tree roots.

WHAT TO LOOK FOR IN BASE-LEVEL STREAMS. Although some base-level streams are darkly stained, most are quite clear enough to be good places for fish watching. Because the shorelines are heavily vegetated, you may have to do your fish watching from a boat. Paddle slowly along the channels, watching for activity close to shore. Look for pale spots on the bottom that could be fish nests. Ease your way into weed beds and keep very quiet. Here is the place to watch small minnows and killifishes being stalked by predators. Pay attention too to the invertebrates that live in the weedy areas.

A Sunny Morning on the Basherkill

About five miles south of the village of Wurtsboro, in southern New York state, a secondary road leaves route 209 and heads east across the Basherkill (Bashakill) swamp. A single-lane bridge across the Basherkill is flanked by pull-off areas where fishers and canoeists launch their boats. Much of this broad U-shaped valley is a flat meadow of Pontederia (pickerel weed), which today is at the peak of its flowering, its deep-blue spikes and heart-shaped leaves crisp and new. Here and there along the road the higher ground is covered with purple loosestrife, also in full flower. The main channel of the stream is clear, but stained the color of root beer. In the shallows near the launching area, dense pond weeds, aquatic buttercup, and bladderwort draped with diaphanous strands of spirogyra struggle to encroach on the channel and add it to their territory. Depressions and openings in the abundant submerged aquatic vegetation appear at first to be empty, but a close look reveals a dense population of small fish that sport a pale stripe between the dark top and sides and a golden line from the tip of the snout to the beginning of the dorsal fin. The fish range in length from two to four inches. At the moment they are aligned to face into the sluggish current, but at the slightest threat they scatter in all directions.

Out in the channel are many slightly smaller fish, also dark on the back and sides. They, too, are holding their own against the current. The fish in the shallows are juvenile creek chubsuckers (Erimyzon oblongus); those in the channel are ironcolor shiners (Notropis chalybaeus). In a few weeks the young chubsuckers will become bottom feeders and their dark side stripes will break up into a series of short vertical bars. The shiners are fully grown and their colors will not change until next spring, when the pale markings of the males will become bright yellow to attract breeding females. The Basherkill is at the northern limit of the ironcolor shiners' range, which extends south to Florida, west along the Gulf Coast, and up the Mississippi Valley to Wisconsin and southwestern Michigan.

Near the bridge there is a fluttering movement in the water. At first it seems to be another school of shiners momentarily struggling against the current, but a closer look reveals that it is a foot-long redfin pickerel hovering two or three inches below the surface. What appeared to be several fish was actually the edges of the pelvic and pectoral fins fluttering as the fish maintained its position in the current. The difficulty of seeing the fish so close to the surface can be traced to a pale reddish stripe down its back, which disrupts the characteristic fish-shaped outline.

*Deeply hidden in the weeds is a dense population of the exquisite blue-spotted sunfish (*Enneacanthus gloriosus*). The tail of this diminutive species is rounded rather than forked. This is another species of the Atlantic coastal plain that is near its northern limit here in the Basherkill. A few years ago a population was discovered in a reservoir near Syracuse, New York. Was this an introduction, the result of an unwitting release of some aquarium pets, or is the reservoir population the remnant of a distribution that was once much wider? We will probably never know for sure, but we do know that a series of specimens in the fish collection of the College of Environmental Science and Forestry of Syracuse University was collected more than sixty years ago in Oneida Lake. If the species was introduced into that part of the country, the introduction must have taken place a long time ago, or perhaps more than once. Perhaps someday forensic techniques of gene sequencing will answer such questions, but for now we can only wonder.*

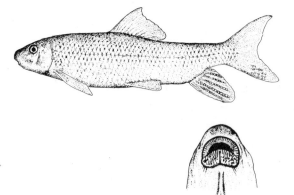

Shorthead redhorse, *Moxostoma macrolepidotum*. Redhorses are nearly round in cross section, but unlike the species of *Catostomus*, they have large scales. Insert: Redhorse suckers have lips with folds. In this species the folds of the lower lips are broken by cross grooves.

Quillback, *Carpiodes cyprinus*. The quillback belongs to the group of suckers that have long dorsal fins and large scales. The high anterior lobe of the dorsal fin gives this species its name.

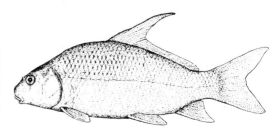

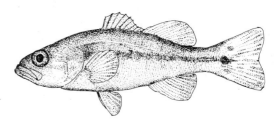

The largemouth bass, *Micropterus salmoides*.

The tadpole madtom, *Noturus gyrinus*. This small species has many short rays at the upper and lower beginnings of the tail fin. As in the rest of the madtoms, the adipose dorsal fin is keellike rather than flaglike.

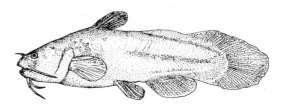

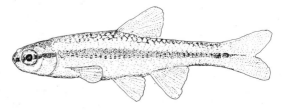

The pugnose shiner, *Notropis anogenis*.

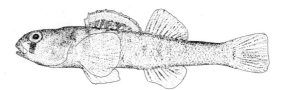

The Iowa darter, *Etheostoma exile*.

Large Rivers

CHARACTERISTICS. Large rivers are navigable streams. Most well-known rivers, such as the Mississippi, Missouri, and Ohio, have been modified by flood-control dams with locks for commercial and recreational boat traffic, and long stretches of their shorelines have been modified by construction or riprap for protection against erosion or by levees for flood containment. Pollution may be severe in some places. Many of the large rivers are interconnected by canal systems.

Larger rivers have locks and dams to allow commercial barge and tug traffic to pass.

There is probably no good definition of a river as opposed to a creek. From the standpoint of the fish, it usually doesn't make much difference how large the stream is, as long as it has a variety of habitats and each habitat is extensive enough to be permanent through dry and wet seasons.

MICROHABITATS. In general, the larger the river, the more microhabitats for fishes. Natural shorelines vary from swampy marshes to clay and shale banks to wooded sections with exposed tree roots and fallen logs. Artificial shorelines range from rock riprap to wood, steel, or concrete bulkheads, dredge spoils, and structures such as piers and bridge pilings. In the open water there may be sandbars,

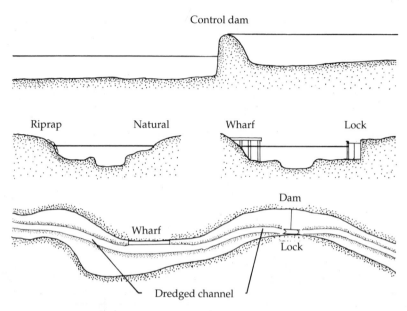

Profile, cross section, and plan of a large river. Navigable rivers are subject to human disturbance and modification in the form of riprap (large stones to prevent erosion) along the shorelines, dredged channels, and locks and control dams to allow large vessels to move up- and downstream.

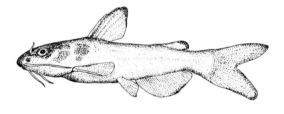

The juvenile channel catfish, *Icta-lurus punctatus.*

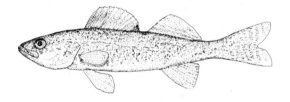

The walleye, *Stizostedion vitreum.*

deltas around the mouths of tributaries, and sharp dropoffs into deep water.

WHAT TO LOOK FOR IN LARGE RIVERS. Large rivers are difficult places to watch fish. They are usually deep and turbid, so it is hard to see fish except when they are in shallow water very close to shore. Boaters and fishers sometimes see gars basking at the surface. Some larger rivers have substantial commercial fisheries for buffalo fish (large suckers), catfish, and perhaps white and yellow bass. If you are just passing by, check the fish markets. If you live in the area, much of your fish watching will be at the end of a fishing pole.

Some of the fishes that are characteristic of large rivers are the alligator gar, paddlefish, channel catfish, blue catfish, blue sucker, flathead catfish, shovelnose and pallid sturgeons, certain plains minnows, and a variety of bass and sunfish.

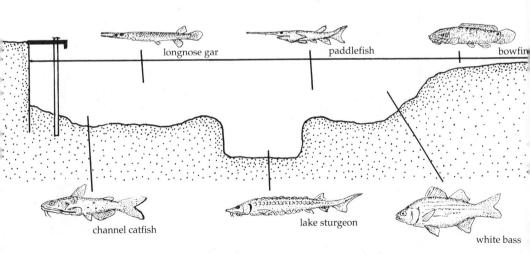

Habitat selection in a large river. Gars stay near the surface and bowfins seek weedy shallows. Paddlefish patrol the open waters feeding on plankton while sturgeons work the deeper parts of the channels. Catfish tend to stay near shelter and white bass patrol open waters near shore.

Estuaries

CHARACTERISTICS. An estuary is a place where fresh and salt water meet. It can be relatively short or more than a hundred miles long. An estuary is a special kind of flowing water environment, transitional between a river and the ocean into which it flows. Near the seashore the bottom of the estuary is actually below sea level. Salt water, being heavier than fresh water, pushes upstream beneath the seaward-flowing fresh water. This intrusion of salt water enables marine species to travel upstream a considerable distance from the ocean. In the typical estuary the limit of the salt front varies with the season and with rainfall upstream in the drainage basin. Some long estuaries have an upriver segment that is entirely fresh water but still is subject to tidal fluctuations. Because estuaries flow across the

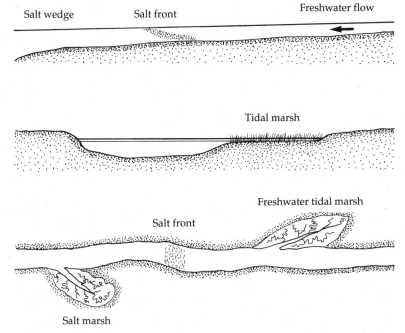

Profile, cross section, and plan of an estuary. Because salt water is denser than fresh water, it tends to push upstream under the fresh water to form a salt front, where salt and fresh water mix. Tidal marshes can be either fresh or salt, depending on the location of the salt front.

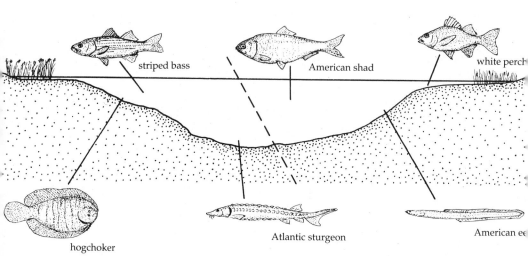

striped bass

American shad

white perch

hogchoker

Atlantic sturgeon

American eel

Habitat selection in an estuary. Striped bass, sturgeons, and shad are anadromous (that is, they swim upstream to spawn) and enter the streams at estuaries. They are found on both sides of the salt front (here indicated by the sloping dashed line). The catadromous eel, which reverses the process and swims to the sea to spawn, moves into the estuary and on up into fresh waters until it is time to return to the sea to spawn. Hogchokers prefer the saltier parts of the estuary. The white perch are truly euryhaline—they are at home in fresh or salt water.

flat coastal plains, they tend to be bordered by marshy wetlands—salt marshes near the coast, freshwater wetlands above the salt front.

MICROHABITATS. The tidal cycles in estuaries create an intertidal zone with microhabitats that do not occur elsewhere. Where the bottom slopes gently, the intertidal zone can be many yards wide, but in areas with steep banks, the intertidal zone is simply a vertical wall. Parts of an estuary may have sand, rock, or mud bottoms, and vegetation may range from marine algae in the lower reaches to cattail marshes upstream.

WHAT TO LOOK FOR IN ESTUARIES. Estuaries are usually quite turbid and not very well suited for fish watching. Sometimes the water is clear in marshes and around the mouths of tributary streams, and these areas are worth checking. In the spring you can sometimes see large schools of alewives or white perch there. Fish frequently break the surface when they are actively feeding or spawning, and observers sometimes see sturgeon weighing a hundred pounds or more basking at the surface, looking like floating logs. The usual ploy of walking the beaches to look for carcasses and talk to fishers may pay off. Species such as the striped bass, shad, and other river herrings enter estuaries to spawn at or above the farthest reach of salt water. Mummichogs, eels, silversides, and white perch live in estuaries' brackish waters throughout the year. Because estuaries are open to the sea, many ocean fishes such as tautog, hakes, and cusk eels stray into their lower reaches from time to time. Many surprises await the angler in the estuary.

Such species as gars, bowfins, freshwater drum, largemouth and smallmouth bass, and large carp may be abundant in the freshwater parts of estuaries. The small sole called the hogchoker is sometimes abundant even well above the salt front.

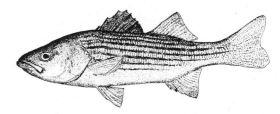

The striped bass, *Morone saxatilis.*

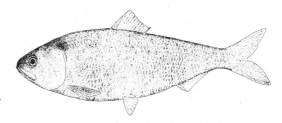

The American shad, *Alosa sapidissima.*

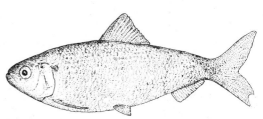

The alewife, *Alosa pseudoharengus.* From a sea-run specimen collected at Cornwall-on-Hudson April 20, 1977. Standard length 262 mm. (AMNH 45522.)

Standing Waters

Lakes, ponds, and open waters of wetlands are collectively called standing waters. Actually the water in such areas is in motion in several ways, so "standing" here does not mean static, it simply means that the waters do not flow.

Standing waters occur in depressions, or basins, and these basins are doomed from the moment they are formed. Eroded sediments and plant remains from the surrounding land are washed in and settle to the bottom along with debris from the resident aquatic plants and animals. Gradually the lake or pond gets shallower until it becomes a wetland. Ultimately it disappears.

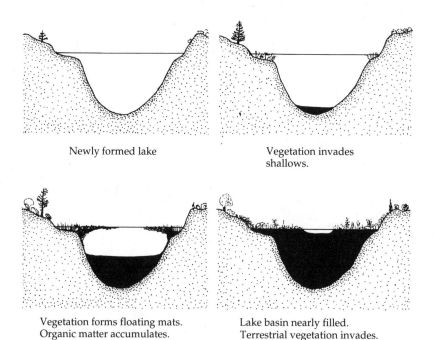

Newly formed lake

Vegetation invades shallows.

Vegetation forms floating mats. Organic matter accumulates.

Lake basin nearly filled. Terrestrial vegetation invades.

Stages in the life and death of a lake. A newly formed lake is colonized by aquatic plants, and gradually the accumulated plant debris, together with sediments washed in from the land, fills the basin. The entire process is known as succession.

Origins of Wetlands, Ponds, and Lakes

As you approach a lake or pond, see if you can figure out how it was originally formed. In mountainous country a lake sometimes forms when a landslide creates a dam across a valley. If this is the case, it will be easy to see where the slide occurred. Some lakes are water-filled volcanic craters.

Natural lakes are abundant in the North but actually quite scarce in the southern parts of the country. Minnesota, not Texas, is the land of lakes. The North owes its lakes to the work of glaciers. As glacial ice pushed southward, it piled up moraines, massive hills of rocks and soil (collectively called glacial till). Some depressions between moraines have been filled with water ever since. The glaciers also scooped out valleys that became lake basins. In mountainous areas, masses of rocks frozen to the bottom of the ice sheet were plucked out as the glacier advanced, leaving depressions that became ponds. As the glaciers receded, debris that washed out of the melting ice filled crevices near the edge of the ice sheet and covered

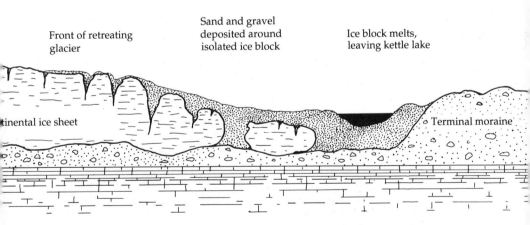

Front of retreating glacier

Sand and gravel deposited around isolated ice block

Ice block melts, leaving kettle lake

tinental ice sheet

Terminal moraine

Formation of a kettle lake. Although the ice sheet continues to flow southward, warming temperatures melt the southernmost ice so that the front of the glacier recedes northward. Crevices near the glacial front widen and become filled with sediments washed out of the ice. Eventually blocks of ice separate from the glacier and become surrounded by glacial sediments, mostly sand and gravel. When these ice blocks finally melt, they leave depressions, or kettles, that become filled with water.

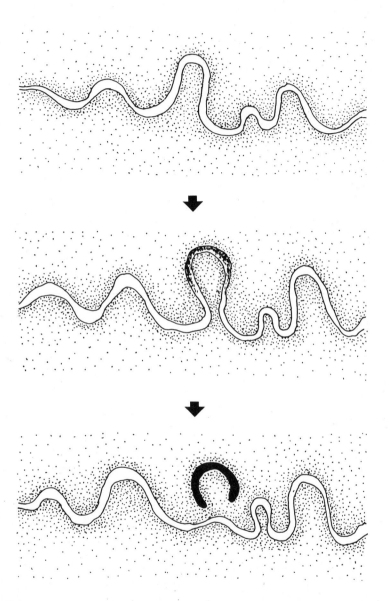

Oxbow lakes are the remnants of old stream meanders. Base-level streams erode the banks on the outsides of the curves while sediments are deposited on the insides of the curves. Over time this process produces deep meanders. Continued erosion cuts off the occasional meander, leaving an oxbow lake.

isolated blocks of melting ice. When these ice blocks finished melting, the resulting depressions became isolated "kettle" lakes, ponds, and wetlands.

South of the area that was covered by the ice sheet, the number of natural lakes declines sharply. Many are "oxbows," formed when rivers changed course and left isolated, cut-off sections.

In some parts of the continent ponds were formed when subterranean chambers collapsed. These sinkholes occur in areas where the underlying bedrock is calcum carbonate limestone. Limestone dissolved as acidic groundwater percolated through cracks and crevices. Gradually the small passages were enlarged into extensive caves. Eventually the roofs of some of the largest chambers collapsed, leaving a depression at the surface. The characteristic land form that results from this subterranean erosion is called Karst topography. In Karst areas even substantial rivers flow underground. This is the habitat of fishes of the family Amblyopsidae, which includes blind cave fishes and two surface-dwelling species.

Over a large part of the country many small ponds accumulate where beavers have built dams. These animals are surprisingly effective at blocking stream courses, and some beaver ponds are home to a varied fish fauna.

Many lakes and ponds have been deliberately constructed for reservoirs, hydroelectric power, flood control, fire protection, or recreational or aesthetic purposes. Impoundments vary from tiny farm ponds to huge reservoirs with hundreds of miles of shoreline. Their shapes reflect the forms of the river valleys that were flooded when the dams were built.

A cross-country flight on a clear day is probably the best way to gain an appreciation for the tremendous number of small farm ponds and reservoirs that exist in North America.

Many ponds along highways were formed when dirt was removed for use in constructing the bed of the highway. These "borrow pits," which often run for miles through lowlands along highways, support large and diverse fish populations.

Thermal Stratification

Ponds and lakes may become thermally stratified during the summer months when warmer and therefore lighter water floats on top of cooler, heavier water. Water is most dense at 4°C (about 39°F). Above and below that temperature, water becomes lighter; that is why ice floats. If ice sank to the bottom, it would be protected from sunlight and never melt, so that in time all northern lakes and ponds would fill up with frozen water and life on this planet would be very different. Four degrees Celsius is indeed a magic number.

As sunlight warms the water near the surface, the water becomes less dense, so that more energy is required for the wind to mix it with deeper, cooler water. Eventually well-defined layers are formed. The warm, less dense surface layer is called the epilimnion; the deep cold layer is called the hypolimnion; and the layer between them is the thermocline. Stratification can also occur in the winter, when a layer of ice prevents the water from mixing. In this case, the upper layer is actually colder than the deep layer; that is, it will be between 0 and 4°C.

It takes a surprising amount of energy to mix water that is thermally stratified in a deep pond or lake—more than the wind can supply throughout most of the year. In the fall, however, the surface temperatures decrease until the temperature and thus the density of the surface water equal those of the lower layers; then it becomes easy for the wind to mix the entire lake. This fall turnover carries well-oxygenated water to the bottom of the lake. Lakes that stratify in the winter have a spring turnover when the temperatures are again uniform. Lakes that are stratified both summer and winter have two turnover periods.

Once stratification is established, there is very little mixing of the layers. Since oxygen diffuses through water very slowly, there is no way to replenish the oxygen that is consumed by organisms in the deeper layers. As a result, oxygen levels drop. In some cases lack of sufficient oxygen may make the lower layers uninhabitable by some species of fishes.

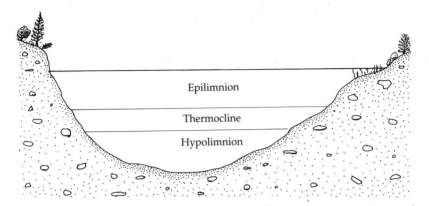

Epilimnion

Thermocline

Hypolimnion

Cross section of a thermally stratified lake. The warmer, less dense epilimnion floats on the cooler, denser hypolimnion. Between them is the thermocline, a layer of rapidly changing temperature.

Shallow bodies of water that are constantly mixed by winds do not stratify, and oxygen absorbed at the surface is carried throughout the water column. Growing plants require sunlight, so lakes with extensive shallow areas can sustain more growing plants than deep lakes with steep sides. Primary productivity is actually measured in grams of carbon that is incorporated into living tissue from atmospheric carbon dioxide.

Even in relatively clear water, however, light doesn't penetrate very far, so rooted plants can grow only in relatively shallow water. Where they do grow, however, they recycle nutrients and produce enormous quantities of living material (biomass), providing food and shelter for many kinds of aquatic plants and animals.

Phytoplankton, tiny floating plants, are also producers. At times they become so abundant that the water looks like green paint. Such blooms are sometime triggered by an excess of nutrients, as when the water is polluted by domestic sewage or fertilizers washed from lawns and fields. Both phytoplankton and larger plants produce large amounts of oxygen when they are exposed to bright sunlight, but on cloudy days they consume more oxygen than they produce, and if they are very abundant they can lower the oxygen content to

the point where both plants and animals suffocate. This is the most common cause of the "summer kill" phenomenon, when large numbers of fishes die.

The quality of standing water, like that of a stream, varies in accordance with the bottom material and the surrounding rock and soils that the water passes over or through on its way to the lake. In recent years many lakes and ponds around the world have had serious problems. The rain that falls over much of the northern hemisphere now contains acid pollutants that result from the burning of fossil fuels. In the past the soils were able to neutralize these acids, but when their capacity was exceeded, the groundwaters suddenly became highly acidic. The problem is especially acute in mountainous areas where rocks have little capacity to neutralize acid to begin with. Many mountain lakes have become unsuited for fish. There is even evidence that some forests are dying as a result of exposure to acid precipitation. Since the acidity comes from the atmosphere, there is no way of tracing it to its source. The task is not to fix blame but to set standards for emissions that will protect the environment. Unfortunately, the corrective measures are costly, and it is difficult to get firms to spend large sums to protect forests that in some cases are thousands of miles from the point of discharge.

Wetlands: Swamps, Marshes, Bogs, and Fens

CHARACTERISTICS. All wetlands are areas that contain substantial amounts of standing water with little flow. Swamps are wetlands with trees. Bogs and fens are vegetated low-lying areas. Bogs have outlets where water from rain runoff and springs flows away. Fens are basins fed by upwelling groundwater. Marshes are usually wetlands dominated by a few species of plants, such as cattails and pickerel weed. Estuarine and saline coastal wetlands are also called marshes. Fens in limestone areas tend to be alkaline.

Some wetlands are small kettle holes; others are the last stages of the process known as succession, which is triggered when aquatic

Fen: fed by groundwater

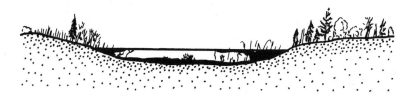

Bog: fed by runoff

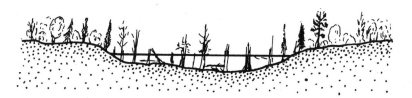

Swamp: wooded wetland

Cross sections of wetlands. Fens are fed primarily by groundwater and bogs are fed by surface runoff. Swamps are wooded wetlands.

plants produce organic material faster than decomposing organisms can recycle it. The remains of the plant bodies gradually accumulate until no open water remains.

MICROHABITATS. Swamps have relatively few kinds of micro-habitat. Tree roots and fallen timber provide cover, and channels in the swamp may have pools and beds of aquatic vegetation. Open waters of bogs and fens may have various kinds of bottoms and patches of aquatic plants. Stands of cattails and sedges also provide cover for fishes. The edges of floating mats of vegetation provide

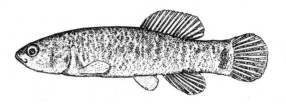

The central mudminnow, *Umbra limi.*

cover, and the roots of floating vegetation are usually excellent hunting grounds for fish that feed on small invertebrates.

WHAT TO LOOK FOR IN WETLANDS.   In the open waters look for minnows, particularly dace in the North. Killifishes and livebearers and mudminnows are also characteristic of wetlands. In the South, sunfishes, pygmy sunfish, pickerels, chubsuckers, and pirate perch are possibilities.

Weed-choked swamps are among the most maligned and mistreated of natural environments. For some reason, a lot of people consider such places repulsive or threatening. Possibly this attitude is a holdover from the days when malaria was prevalent, and the only

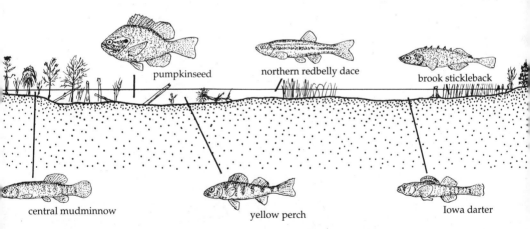

Wetlands, from wooded swamps to open fens, are home to a few species of fishes that can tolerate low oxygen levels. Yellow perch and pumpkinseed sunfish can be found in the more open areas. Mudminnows and brook sticklebacks seek shelter in weedy areas. The Iowa darter can be found in more open areas of flocculent bottom.

way to control it was to drain swamps so that the disease-carrying mosquitos had no place to breed.

How anyone can fail to see beauty in a field of blue-flowered pickerel weed or swaying cattail is a mystery to me. Beneath the surface, graceful stands of waterweeds—coontail, bladderwort, hornwort, potamogetons, elodea—combine to produce some of the most elegant surrealist scenery on this planet. Swamps are rich in species, rich in biomass. Leeches and a few minor insect bites are a small price to pay for a visit to this little-known realm of exquisite loveliness.

Ponds and Small Lakes

CHARACTERISTICS. A pond is a body of standing water that is too small to have a wave-swept beach. As in the case of other habitats, there is no sharp division between ponds and lakes.

Like streams, lakes and ponds are extremely diverse. In addition to their overall size, standing waters vary greatly in basin shape, in the ratio of shoreline to surface area, in their flushing rate (a measure of how long the average drop of water remains in the lake before being carried downstream), and in the temperature, color, and chemical composition of their waters. The area of the drainage basin and the contours of the surrounding land profoundly affect the characteristics of the lake or pond, and of course the human population along the shoreline and in the surrounding countryside influences them in many ways. All of these factors combine to determine what organisms can live there.

MICROHABITATS. Even small ponds may have several kinds of shoreline, marshy in some areas, wooded or rocky in others. Shallows may have a sand, rock, or mud floor. Most small ponds contain fallen trees and logs, and some have islands of floating vegetation. Be sure to check out the marshy shoreline and patches of aquatic vegetation.

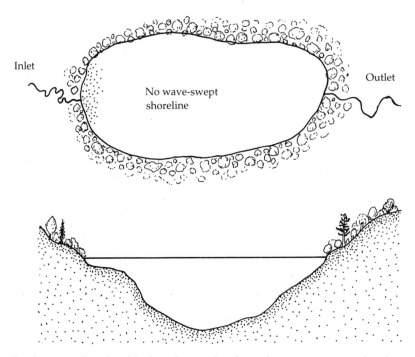

Inlet

No wave-swept
shoreline

Outlet

Ponds are small enclosed bodies of water that do not have a wave-swept shoreline.

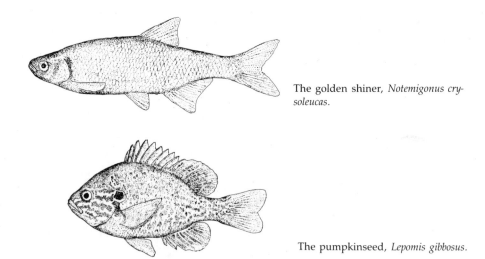

The golden shiner, *Notemigonus crysoleucas*.

The pumpkinseed, *Lepomis gibbosus*.

WHAT TO LOOK FOR IN PONDS AND SMALL LAKES. Along the shoreline look for minnows and killifishes. In the South look for livebearers (family Poeciliidae). Sunfishes are often abundant in ponds, and in the North you will find perch and a few darters, such as the johnny darter and the Iowa darter.

Bullheads are often abundant in ponds but they are rather reclusive and may not be seen except when they are caught by anglers or during the spring and summer, when they are herding their young.

Northern ponds may support populations of brook trout, and some have chain, grass, or redfin pickerel. Borrow pits in the South often have gars and bowfins.

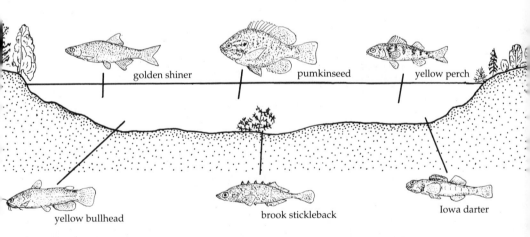

Ponds and small lakes are home to pumpkinseed sunfish, yellow perch, and golden shiners, which select open waters. Bullheads, sticklebacks, and Iowa darters tend to be bottom dwellers.

Large Lakes

CHARACTERISTICS. A lake differs from a pond in that at least part of its shoreline is a wave-swept beach. These bodies of water range in size from a few acres to hundreds of square miles. The Great Lakes are so large that they have minuscule tides. Most larger lakes are thermally stratified during at least part of the year, although some warm shallow lakes in the South are completely mixed throughout the year, and a few special lakes are always stratified.

Many lakes are really large reservoirs formed or deepened by dams across streams. Reservoirs are sometimes subject to great variations in depth as water is released or diverted to generate electric power, to provide drinking water, or to maintain water levels for navigation. During the drier parts of the year many reservoirs have vast areas of exposed lake bottom.

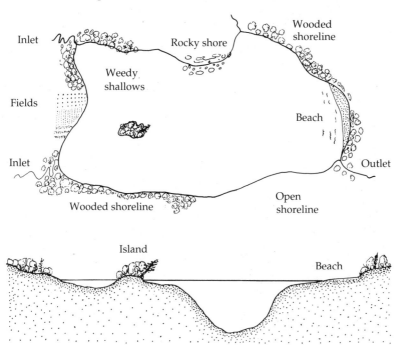

A lake is an enclosed body of water that is large enough to have a wave-swept shoreline. Most lakes have several kinds of shoreline and may have deep and shallow areas.

Any very large lake is subject to an occasional seiche, a disturbance of the surface caused by winds that blow the water from one end of the lake to the other. When the wind blows along the axis of a large lake for a few hours, the water level can change two or three feet or more. After a seiche is established, the water oscillates between one end of the lake and the other. The effect is similar to that of a tide in the sea, but seiches have no regular rhythm; they occur at the whim of the wind.

MICROHABITATS. Large lakes can have complex shorelines with weedy bays and backwaters. Sometimes a backwater is almost cut off by a highway or railroad. Lakes have the kinds of shorelines seen around ponds, and beaches besides. Some species of fish spend much of their time feeding in the smooth bottom shallows just off-shore from the beaches.

WHAT TO LOOK FOR IN LARGE LAKES. Along sandy beaches look for schools of small minnows and occasional baby bullheads. In the spring or early summer look for logperch and, at night, trout-perch. Rocky shorelines shelter bass, catfishes, white suckers, perch, rock bass, and other sunfishes.

Weedy shorelines are good places to see bowfins, gars, carp, and

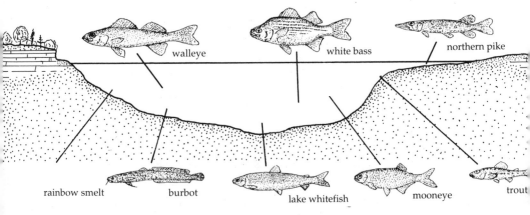

Habitat selection in a lake. Large lakes offer many habitats, some similar to those of large rivers and others like those of ponds. Among the larger fishes of deep waters in large lakes are the lake whitefish, the burbot, and the mooneyes. Walleyes in open waters, white bass near shore, and northern pike are favorite game fish. Among the more interesting smaller species are the smelt and the trout-perch.

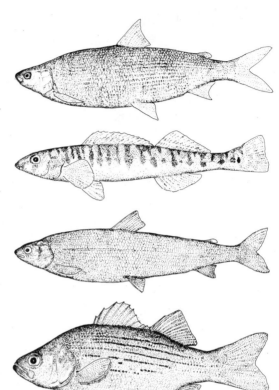

The lake whitefish, *Coregonus clupea-formis.*

The logperch, *Percina caprodes.*

The round whitefish, *Prosopium cylindraceum.*

The white bass, *Morone chrysops.*

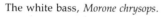

goldfish spawning, sunfish nests, sticklebacks, yellow perch, and pikes and pickerels lurking in the clearer water.

The deeper parts of lakes harbor the more interesting and distinctive species, but it is usually not possible to do much fish watching in the deeper parts of large lakes unless you are a scuba diver. To see these species you will have to rely on anglers, fish markets, and occasional carcasses washed up on beaches. Sturgeons, mooneye and goldeye, alewives and large gizzard shads, deepwater sculpins, walleyes, large burbots, rainbow smelts, salmons, whitefishes, lake herring, and lake trouts make the deep-lake fauna distinctive.

Some large deep lakes are said to be the homes of unknown "monsters" that appear from time to time in blurry photographs taken in poor light. Of course you don't believe in that sort of thing, but that's no reason not to keep an eye out for them.

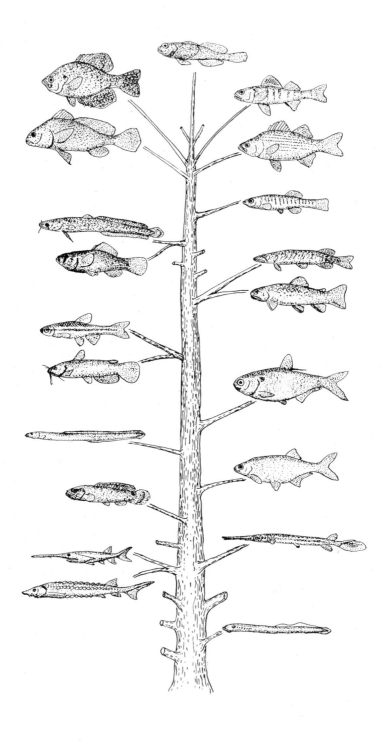

4   *The Fishes*

The following pages offer a brief introduction to the families of fishes that live east of the Rocky Mountains, with emphasis on those that may be seen in shallow water. Although I really know better (see appendix 1), I include the lampreys, which are particularly fascinating aquatic vertebrates. The families are arranged in conventional phylogenetic order—that is, from the most general to the most specialized. Remember, though, that species assigned to general groups can have some very specialized features.

The fish watcher will be concerned mostly with families. In the field it is often possible to see that a particular fish is a catfish but we may not be able to see the features that would tell us which catfish it is. Our field notes will frequently have such entries as "Bullhead, species not determined" or "Salmonid." Families, however, are themselves grouped into "higher" groups, and a familiarity with these higher groups often helps to sort things out in our minds. Therefore I have included in appendix 1 brief characterizations of some of the important "higher groups." These are the basis of the "tree" at the beginning of this chapter.

Fish Anatomy

A few technical terms are necessary if you are going to communicate with other fish watchers, or even with your own notebook. At

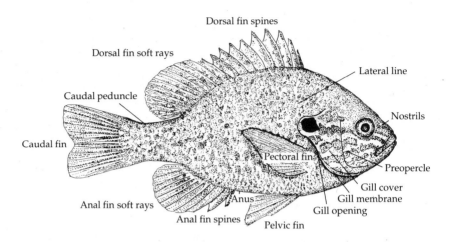

External anatomy of the pumpkinseed.

the very least, you need to know the names of the fins and a few other landmarks that have no exact counterparts in human anatomy. The standard number of fins is seven: two pectoral fins, two pelvic fins, a dorsal fin, an anal fin, and a caudal fin. But some fish have more and some have fewer.

The upper side of the fish when it is in its normal swimming position is the dorsal side. Any fins on its back are therefore called the dorsal fins. The belly side is the ventral side and the paired pelvic fins, sometimes called ventral fins in older books, lie ahead of the anus. The anal fin is just behind the anus. The caudal fin is the tail. The pectoral or shoulder fins are located just behind the gill opening.

There are three kinds of fins. Soft-rayed fins are supported by bony rods that are segmented so that they are quite flexible. Soft fin rays are usually, but not always, branched. Spiny fins are supported by harder, unsegmented and unbranched spines. If both spines and rays are present, the spines will be located at the anterior (front) end of the fin. An adipose fin, as its name implies, is a fatty keel that has no bony supports at all. Adipose fins are found in trouts, salmons, whitefishes, catfishes, and trout-perch on the dorsal midline, just anterior to the tail.

A fish's head is considered to end at the gill opening. The plate that protects the gills is called the gill cover or operculum. Along its ventral edge is a membrane supported by bony rods called branchiostegal rays. This branchiostegal membrane acts as a sort of check valve to ensure that when the fish breathes, the water flows in through the mouth and out through the gill opening. On the side of the head, just in front of the operculum, is a superficial bone called the preopercle. The preopercle usually has a free edge and sometimes its margin has spines or small serrations. In all fish except sturgeons and lampreys, the upper jaw consists of two pairs of bones, the premaxillae and the maxillae. These bones are more or less movable. In higher fish the premaxilla extends backward to form the edge of the mouth. There may be other patches of teeth on the roof of the mouth.

If you lift the gill cover and look inside, you will find four gill arches on each side. Each gill arch is supported by a series of bones, and bears two rows of gill filaments on its outer posterior side. On its anterior side it has a series on short bony processes called gill rakers, which form a sort of grating that keeps prey from escaping through the gill opening. Gill rakers tend to be numerous, long, and slender in fishes that feed on small planktonic organisms; they are shorter, stouter, and fewer in carnivorous species.

The part of the fish that supports the tail is called the caudal peduncle. In the bowfin and some other fish it bears distinctive color marks. If the caudal peduncle is very slender, the fish is a stickleback.

The scales of most fishes overlap like shingles on a roof. Scales are embedded in the skin and covered by a thin layer of epidermis. Scales grow by adding connective tissue and bony ridges to their outer margins. Gaps in the bony ridges allow the scale to flex. There are several kinds of scales. In cycloid scales the exposed part is pretty much like the rest of the scale, and fish with cycloid scales feel smooth. Ctenoid scales have small teeth on the part that is exposed, and fishes with ctenoid scales are rough to the touch, even through their usual coat of slime. The slime, incidentally, is the fish's chief protection against infection. Ganoid scales, found in gars, are flint-hard diamond-shaped plates that overlap only slightly. Bowfins have a fourth kind of scale in which the bony ridges are straight instead of circular. In addition to these main types, sturgeons have five rows of large, thick bony plates along the body, with smaller plates between them. Bony plates are also found in some stickle-backs. Catfishes have no scales, eels have embedded scales that do not overlap, and burbots have a peculiar kind of scale unlike any of the others.

The size of the scales is one of the best means to tell some species apart. Scale size is measured by counts; the higher the count, the smaller the scales. The commonly used count is the number of scales in the lateral line or along the middle of the side of the body from the gill cover to the base of the tail fin. Sometimes diagonal counts—for example, the number of scales between the lateral line and the base of the dorsal fin—are useful.

Some special terms are used to describe the shapes of fish. If the fish is round in cross section, it is said to be *terete*. If it is flattened from side to side, it is *compressed,* and if it is flattened dorsoventrally, it is *depressed*. Body depth is the distance from the dorsal midline to the ventral midline. Thus a compressed fish can be deep-bodied or it can be ribbon-like.

Some conventional terms also describe color patterns. If the body is striped and the stripes run vertically, the fish is said to be *banded.* If the stripes run longitudinally, the fish is *striped* or, if the stripes are narrow, *lined*. Spots are distinct and more or less regular; blotches are more diffuse, with irregular outlines. Spots surrounded by a ring of contrasting color are said to be *ocellated*. Sometimes you can describe colors quite accurately by comparing them with a chart provided by a paint manufacturer and available at a hardware store.

One more thing: Scientists usually use standard length, which is the distance from the tip of the snout to the base of the tail—not to the tip. The principal reason is that tails frequently get broken when fish are caught. Because this measure is shorter than the total length, it is not popular with anglers.

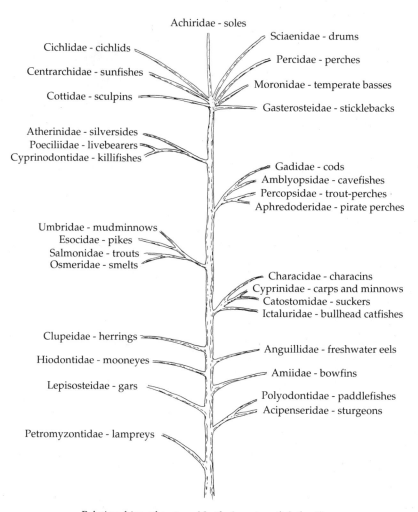

Relationships of eastern North American fish families.

Lampreys
(Family Petromyzontidae)

Lampreys are eel-shaped fishes with no jaws, paired fins, or scales. Our species all have seven pairs of external gill openings. The mouth is circular, sucker-like, partly or completely lined with horny teeth. The color is silvery, gray, or brown mottled with yellow.

The silver lamprey, *Ichthyomyzon unicuspis,* is one of the native North American parasitic species of lamprey. The insert shows the teeth lining the mouth cavity and the bladelike cutting and scraping teeth on the tongue in the center of the disk.

The mouth of ammocoetes, the larval lamprey. The ammocoetes has no developed eyes and the mouth is shielded by a fleshy hood. Fringed tentacles screen food particles drifting by.

Lampreys are among the longest lived of all our fishes. In the larval stage, called ammocoetes, the eyes are undeveloped and the mouth is surrounded by feathery tentacles and protected by a hoodlike structure. The ammocoetes lives in soft mud and feeds on detritus and drifting organisms. After four years or longer, it develops the eyes, fins, gonads, and other organs of an adult and drifts downstream, where it becomes parasitic on other fishes. Six to eighteen months later, it matures and ascends the stream to spawn. Having spawned, it dies. Some species have secondarily lost the ability to feed as parasites. In these species the gut degenerates at the time the ammocoetes is transformed into an adult, and thereafter it does not feed. It manages to live just the same.

Lampreys have a bad reputation because of their parasitic lifestyle. The best-known lamprey, the sea lamprey (*Petromyzon marinus*), is found on both sides of the Atlantic Ocean. In Europe it is a valued commercial food fish but it is not eaten in the Americas, although the larval stages are sometimes used for live bait. Sea lampreys became established in the upper Great Lakes (those above Niagara Falls) after the Welland Canal was opened in 1824. After a slow passage through Lake Erie they became extremely abundant in Lakes Huron and Michigan in the 1930s and contributed to the destruction of the commercial fishery in those lakes. In all fairness, it must be pointed out that the lamprey didn't kill the fishery all by itself. Overfishing and silting of the spawning grounds had already hurt the populations, and the lamprey simply came along in time to finish the job in the 1930s and 1940s.

Sea lampreys are controlled by selective poisoning of the larvae in the streams. The goal is to reduce the populations so that other fishes can thrive, but it probably never will be possible to eradicate the sea lamprey completely. Unfortunately, the poison also kills native species of lampreys that are important natural components of our fauna.

Adult lampreys move into small streams to spawn during the late spring and early summer. Their habitat requirements are quite strict: they require gravel of a particular size, and the water current must move at a rate of at least 2 to 4 feet per second. They build nests by moving pebbles to hollow out a shallow depression. After spawning they die. A large sea lamprey can lay more than a million eggs. After the eggs hatch, the larvae leave the gravel and drift downstream to burrow in the mud, leaving only their heads sticking out. They spend from four to eight or more years in the larval stage, feeding on plankton and organic matter that they trap with their feather-like tentacles. Finally they are transformed into adults. Their eyes become visible and the reproductive organs develop. The hood around the mouth disappears and the tentacles shrink so that the mouth becomes a shallow sucker-like disk. Horny teeth develop around the mouth and on the tongue.

After their transformation the adult sea lampreys seek hosts. They attach themselves to other fishes, rasp their way through the host's skin with their tongues, and feed on the blood and lymph from the wound. In three to nine days the host fish can be nearly dead. When one host becomes weak or dies, the sea lamprey leaves it to find another host. This procedure is repeated over the next three to fifteen months. Sometimes sea lampreys in the Great Lakes attach themselves to human swimmers whose skin temperature has been lowered to fish level by exposure to cold water. In late summer sea lampreys gather around the mouths of streams and in early spring they begin to move upstream to sites suitable for spawning.

Several smaller parasitic species are native to our inland streams. The silver lamprey, the Ohio lamprey, and the chestnut lamprey are all parasitic, but they are small and relatively unknown. There are also several nonparasitic species, among them the northern brook lamprey, the mountain brook lamprey, and the American brook lamprey. Nonparasitic species simply do not feed after they are transformed from the larval stage.

Lamprey nests can be seen in a number of streams. Carp River, in the northern part of Michigan's lower peninsula, just outside the entrance to Wilderness State Park, is a good place to see them in early June, and the Delaware River below the dam near Downsville, New York, usually has huge sea lampreys on the nests during the first week of June. The nest depressions are up to two feet across and buttressed by crescent-shaped piles of stones up to four or five inches in diameter. Adults on the nests are fearless and can often be caught by hand, although they are nearly impossible to hold on to. Larvae can be scooped out of muddy areas with a dip net.

East Branch of the Delaware River, June 8, 1980

It's a little gloomy for a June day. The skies are overcast with a gray blanket and there's a light breeze. About three miles south of the town of Downsville we turn onto an unused section of old route 30, a sort of terrestrial oxbow left when the highway was straightened in the name of progress. After parking our van next to a pile of concrete road debris, we grab armloads of equipment and crash our way down a wooded embankment to the edge of the river. With more enthusiasm than good sense I wade out to begin the search for lamprey nests. I am about three minutes ahead of the others, time enough to realize the error of my judgment. This water is too cold for wet wading. I return to the shore and we all head back to the van and struggle into our waders. On the second try things go better. The waders leak a little, but the trapped water soon warms to a tolerable level. The stream is about 75 feet wide at this point and about 2 feet deep or a little deeper. The current is moderately swift but presents no real problem. While I cross to the spot where I saw the lampreys last year, my companions work downstream toward a double riffle where the stream divides to circle a small island. I am disappointed to find none of the nests that were so prominent before. I had been sure the lampreys would be here a week earlier than last year, when we found only empty nests and dead bodies.

Suddenly a shriek tells me that our sharp-eyed geology student has found a lamprey. I hurry as fast as water and waders permit, and when I am still twenty feet away I see that she has indeed located a lamprey—and what a lamprey! Although I have often seen landlocked sea lampreys in northern Michigan, they were nothing like the monster confronting us now. Close to 2 feet long and 2 inches thick, this lamprey must have spent at least a full year and a half in the ocean before starting its journey to the ancestral spawning ground. This one is a male, as evidenced by its splotched yellow-orange color and the thick fatty ridge in front of its dorsal fin. Females are mottled gray and lack the dorsal ridge, although they do have a fleshy keel in front of the anal opening.

This year we are too early. The only sign of nests is a few shallow depressions, and we find no pairs, only single individuals. In another few days we would have been able to watch as they tugged away at the stones, moving them downstream into a crescent-shaped mound, and taking time out every few minutes for a brief spawning episode. Once the cycle starts, it will be repeated until the adults are spent and ready to die in peace, leaving the next generation snug in their stony homes.

Sturgeons
(Family Acipenseridae)

Sturgeons are primitive bony fishes with fins supported by horny fin rays, like those of sharks. The tail is heterocercal—that is, asymmetrical—with the backbone curved upward into the dorsal lobe. The lower lobe of the tail merely consists of longer rays. The body has five rows of bony plates so that it is pentagonal in cross section. The dorsal, anal, and pelvic fins are far back on the body, and the mouth is located on the underside of the head.

The Atlantic sturgeon, *Acipenser oxy-rhynchus*, is unmistakable with its five rows of bony plates and fins resembling those of sharks. The mouth (insert) can be extended into a tube for feeding on the bottom.

Most of us will have little chance of seeing a sturgeon alive unless we are in one of those areas of the country where the sturgeons are so abundant that a fishery has been established for them. Even then we probably will see them only after they have been caught. In some areas, however, sturgeons are speared through the ice as they make their way to the spawning grounds, and presumably a dedicated fish watcher could cut a hole in the ice to observe them as they move upstream.

Sometimes dead sturgeons wash up on beaches and we can get an opportunity to see these fascinating fish close up. There is no mistaking a sturgeon. Perhaps the most obvious thing about it is the rows of bony plates along the body. Each plate is exquisitely sculptured, and in young fish a central keel supports a definite point or spine. As the fish gets older, the plates become smoother, but they retain a surface texture of ridges surrounding shallow pits. The ventral rows of plates become quite eroded in older fish and sometimes even appear to be absent. Smaller plates are embedded in the skin between the rows of plates.

The head of the sturgeon is covered with bony plates as well. The gill cover seems to be too small and there is usually a gap through which the gill can be seen. On the underside of the snout there are two pairs of feathery barbels somewhat ahead of the mouth. These have sensitive chemoreceptors—taste buds, really—and are one of the main systems sturgeons use to locate their food. The sturgeon's eyes are rather poorly developed. Its mouth is pretty spectacular. It has no teeth, but it can be extended into a tube to slurp in food as the sturgeon cruises the bottom like a self-propelled vacuum cleaner. Its food consists of bottom-dwelling organisms and other organic matter.

Sturgeons are big-water fish. They live in large rivers and lakes, and some species are anadromous, spending most of their life in the ocean but returning to fresh water to spawn. In North America the genus *Scaphirhynchus* consists of the freshwater pallid sturgeon in the Mississippi system, the shovelnose sturgeon in the Mississippi and a few other rivers flowing into the Gulf of Mexico, and a recently described species. These three species have rather slender caudal peduncles with flattened, shovel-shaped heads. The rest of our species belong to the genus *Acipenser,* which has one freshwater species plus two anadromous species, one on each coast. The pallid and shovelnose sturgeons reach lengths of only about 5 and 3 feet, respectively, but the lake sturgeon can grow to 8 feet or so and the Atlantic sturgeon close to 12 feet. On the East Coast the Atlantic sturgeon is a commercial species but the smaller shortnose is quite scarce and is on the federal list of endangered species. A size limit of 48 inches protects the shortnose, which doesn't get that large, and allows more Atlantic sturgeons to reach maturity before they are harvested.

Sturgeons grow slowly, and Atlantic sturgeons do not mature until they are between 10 and 20 years old. Atlantic sturgeons were once so abundant that work crews objected to being fed sturgeon more than a few times a week, but by the turn of the century their numbers had been so greatly reduced that they were commercially extinct. Since then the populations have been recovering slowly, but they must be monitored closely and the take is strictly limited. The meat is especially good smoked and the eggs are used to make caviar.

Lake sturgeons reproduce early in the spring, moving into shallows or ascending streams until they encounter a barrier. The eggs are simply scattered; the sturgeon builds no nest.

Some years ago my students and I came upon the carcass of a large lake sturgeon washed up on the beach of an island in Lake Erie where the population is so low that it is doubtful that sturgeons are still reproducing. The sight of the remains of this magnificent fish, recently dead but representing a population that had been doomed for many years, was a potent emotional lesson in the meaning of the words "endangered species."

Paddlefishes
(Family Polyodontidae)

Paddlefishes are highly specialized sturgeons that have lost their bony plates and have a long, flat, spatula-shaped snout. Like other sturgeons, they have fins that resemble those of sharks. The gill cover is very long, flexible, and gracefully pointed. There are only two paddlefish species in the world, one in North America, the other in China. Their teeth are minute, sandpaper-like denticles.

The paddlefish, *Polyodon spathula*, which can weigh 100 pounds or more, is one of the most improbably animals in North America. Its most conspicuous feature is its flat, spatula-shaped snout, which accounts for fully one-third of the length of the body in small juveniles, somewhat less in larger individuals. It has an enormous mouth, a long pointed flexible gill cover, and numerous long, slender gill rakers. All of these features are adaptations for feeding on plankton, which the paddlefish catches by straining large quantities of water through its gill rakers. The paddle is a sensitive tactile organ used for locating swarms of its microscopic prey. It is not, as some people have thought, used as a shovel.

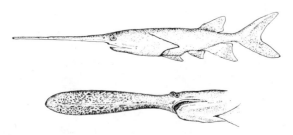

Despite the lack of bony plates and the spatula-shaped snout, the fins of the paddlefish, *Polyodon spathula*, reveal its close relationship to the sturgeons. The insert shows the snout in oblique ventral view.

If you overlook these obvious specializations and the fact that the paddlefish has no bony plates, it is quite similar to the sturgeons. It even has barbels on the underside of the snout, but they are very tiny and easily overlooked. When the paddlefish is first hatched, the resemblance is striking; the paddle is undeveloped and the snout is conical, so the larvae look very much like tiny sturgeons.

Paddlefish have fins like those of sturgeons and sharks and their tails are strongly heterocercal, although the rays that form the lower lobe are so long that the lobes of the tail look nearly symmetrical. In fact, the fins of paddlefish are so much like those of sharks that when it was first discovered it was placed in the same genus as the common dogfish shark. Because these fish have no scales and are similar in color to some catfishes, they are sometimes called "spoon-bill cats."

Paddlefishes are confined to larger rivers draining into the Gulf of Mexico. They are seldom seen, but at night they sometimes swim near the surface, feeding on swarms of plankton.

Louisiana, 1950

We are camped along the Pearl River where it separates Louisiana from Mississippi. This is a typical southern river, rather swift and muddy with high soil banks and many trees that have been undermined by the current until they have fallen into the river, where they remain with their roots still clinging to the bank.

We are part of a survey of the amphibians and reptiles of Louisiana and we have come to spend a few days collecting in this extreme eastern part of the state. Our particular emphasis this trip is on turtles, especially map turtles of the genus Graptemys, *because there is some question as to the relationships of their populations along the Gulf Coast. Earlier we discovered that young map turtles spend the night sprawled out just below the water's surface on logs that extend out into the river. By cruising along the bank in a small outboard boat we can ease the bow in to shore along the logs, and if we are careful we can get close enough to pick up the turtles by hand. Once in awhile a water snake gets shaken into the boat from overhanging branches, but we are used to snakes by now.*

Tonight we have decided to try our luck in a small oxbow (a loop of the river that temporarily has been cut off from the main stream). Rather than manhandle our outboard into the oxbow, we are using an ancient rowboat that we found already there. Our first catch is a baby alligator with one foot missing. Blinded by our lights, he simply freezes, and we easily pick him up and stuff him into a large canvas collecting bag. Suddenly we become aware of some fair-sized vague fish shapes swimming around the boat. As we look closer, some of them come nearer to the surface, and suddenly we can see that they are paddlefish. They are swimming more or less randomly, apparently feeding on plankton near the surface. Later we will wonder if the plankton was attracted by our lights and in turn attracted the paddlefish. Earlier we came across a commercial gill net with some large paddlefish in it, and it occurs to us that a paddlefish or two would be a welcome addition to our diet, so we return to shore to get a spear. Back at the oxbow we turn the boat around so that one person can sit on the bow and paddle the boat like a canoe while the other can move the width of the stern for good shots with the spear. Pretty clumsy, but speed is not important here. In a short time we have a couple of two-foot-long paddlefish, quite enough for a good meal.

Gars
(Family Lepisosteidae)

Gars are elongate fishes with hard, diamond-shaped scales and elongate jaws with pointed teeth. Their fins are supported by bony rays and the dorsal and anal fins are set far back on the body. Gars have rounded, abbreviate heterocercal tails, the upper base longer than the lower. The swim bladder serves as a functional lung. The

This juvenile longnose gar, *Lepisosteus osseus*, has bold color markings that serve as camouflage by making the fish look like a floating twig. Specimen from Burt Lake, Michigan, August 1980.

upper jawbone is rigidly attached to the skull, not capable of independent motion. Gars are found only in North and Central America and in Cuba.

The naturalist Archie Carr once described gars as having a "paleozoic leer." With their long, toothy jaws and armor-plate scales, gars do look like fossils come alive. They are among the most primitive of the bony fishes. Their tails, for example, are turned slightly upward in an abbreviated form of the strongly upturned tails of sturgeons, and young gars up to 6 or 8 inches long have long dorsal filament-like remnants of the heterocercal tail. Unlike sturgeons, however, gars have bony, well-separated fin rays.

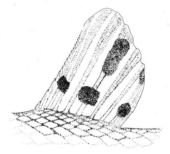

The leading edge of the dorsal fin of the longnose gar, *Lepisosteus osseus*, has characteristic scales called fulcra.

Gars are sometimes called gar-pikes, presumably because their toothy jaws and arrow-shaped bodies suggest the true pikes and pickerels, which are more modern fishes. Linnaeus, the first modern classifier of fishes, was so impressed by the jaw similarities that he placed the gars and pikes together, and threw in the marine needle-fishes to boot. Today we have ample evidence that these three groups of fishes are not at all closely related.

Gars are often seen near the surface. They usually stalk their prey, then kill with a quick sideways sweep of their jaws. Young gars are darker than the silvery-gray adults and look for all the world like floating twigs with teeth.

Gars are air breathers and are much given to jumping and creating a fuss at the surface. They can actually drown if they are confined in low-oxygen water without access to the surface. They inhabit the weedy areas of lakes and slower rivers as far north as southern

Canada, although they are usually thought of as southern fishes. About seven species of gars live in North and Central America and Cuba. The largest species is the alligator gar, which lives in the lower Mississippi and other Gulf Coast drainages south into Mexico. It can reach lengths of close to 10 feet.

Gars are hardy fish, and a small one can be kept in an aquarium as long as one is willing to supply it with small fish for food. Some anglers fish for gars with hooks or wire nooses attached to gloating jugs or poles. After the fish hooks itself, the angler is in for a high-speed pursuit as he tries to catch up with his quarry. The flint-hard, diamond-shaped scales of gars are exceptionally attractive and are sometimes used to make jewelry.

One thing, though—gar eggs don't make good caviar; they are extremely toxic.

Bowfin
(Family Amiidae)

Bowfins are heavy-bodied fishes with a long, wavy dorsal fin and a slightly asymmetrical tail. The head is bullet-shaped with a large bony plate between the lower jaws and large plates at the sides. They have rather small eyes, and the anterior nostrils are at the ends of short tubes. The only living species of bowfin occurs naturally only in North America.

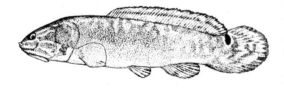

The bowfin, *Amia calva,* is a heavy-bodied fish with a long, wavy dorsal fin. Its bullet-shaped head has heavy plates behind the eye and a characteristic gular plate under the lower jaw.

The bowfin is a rather primitive fish. One of its most conspicuous features is the gular plate, the bony shield on the chin between the lower jawbones. Most of the higher fishes have lost the gular plate. Bowfins also have a primitive type of rather large rectangular scales with longitudinal ridges. Like the gars, bowfins have abbreviate heterocercal tails, holdovers from the heterocercal tails of their ancestors. The tail itself is nearly symmetrical, but the backbone turns upward and the upper base of the fin is longer than the lower.

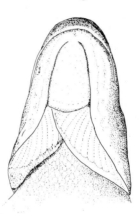

Bowfins have a bony gular plate between the lower jaws.

Actually bowfins are rather attractive, if ungraceful, fishes. Females tend to be a rather drab grayish green, but the males, which are smaller, are quite colorful, especially during the spring breeding season, when their lower fins turn brilliant green and the entire ventral surface becomes turquoise. Both sexes have some yellow and black stripes on the head and a large dark spot on the upper base of the tail. This spot is set off by a bright yellow border in the males, but in the females the yellow ring is absent and the spot is more diffuse.

Bowfins are thought of as fish of the South, where they live in bayous and borrow pits, but they range as far north as southern Michigan and Lakes Ontario and Champlain in the Northeast. They live in quiet, weedy areas, and they are voracious predators. Their flesh is rather soft so they are not considered desirable food fish, although Dr. Brooks Burr informs me that year after year college students invariably place bowfins first in blind taste tests. Bowfins are often considered to be trash fish, but in fact they probably play an important role in keeping some other prolific species from overpopulation and stunting.

Bowfins are the sole surviving members of a group of fishes that has a reasonably good fossil record. Their breeding habits, too, make them interesting to watch. They spawn in the spring—in May in southern Michigan—and the males move into shallows to prepare nests, which are shallow depressions among the remains of aquatic plants that grew during the previous summer. After a brief and direct courtship, the female deposits her eggs in the nest and leaves. The male remains to guard the eggs and, later, the young until they get large enough to scatter. When the young first hatch, they are jet black and have adhesive sucker organs on their snouts. They remain attached to the plant debris in the nest until their yolk supply is nearly gone and they have to begin feeding on their own. After they start to feed, their color becomes lighter. By mid-June the schools break up, although you may see a young bowfin along the shore, and you can spook a larger one almost any time you poke your canoe into a marshy area.

One more thing: Bowfins are air breathers. Their swim bladders are chambered so they can gulp air and use it to supplement the oxygen their gills extract from the water. This arrangement lets them thrive in waters where decaying plant debris sometimes uses up the oxygen so that fishes without the ability to breathe air would suffocate. Is it any wonder that the bowfin has survived beyond its time?

Mooneye and Goldeye
(Family Hiodontidae)

The mooneye and goldeye look a lot like herrings but they do not have saw-edged bellies and are actually members of a group of fishes called the Osteoglossomorpha (bony tongues and feather backs), which is confined mostly to Africa, South America, and Southeast Asia. The mooneye and goldeye are its only representatives in North America.

These silvery, compressed fishes have large eyes and short snouts. They have no adipose fins and no fin spines. The tail is forked, the pelvic fins are abdominal, and the anal fin is much longer than the

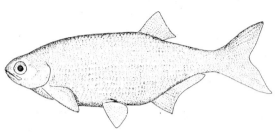

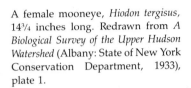

A female mooneye, *Hiodon tergisus,* 14¾ inches long. Redrawn from *A Biological Survey of the Upper Hudson Watershed* (Albany: State of New York Conservation Department, 1933), plate 1.

dorsal fin. Their most important characteristic is that they have a band of large teeth on the mid-line of the roof of the mouth, opposed by equally impressive teeth on the tongue and floor of the mouth. Mooneye and goldeye are big-water fishes of central North America. The goldeye is a commercial species in Canada, where it is smoked. The flesh is not particularly good, and the earliest use was for dog food. Smoking improves the flavor and has led to some popularity. Originally the goldeyes were smoked over willow fires, which gave them a yellow color. As willow wood became scarce, oak was substituted, and the fish were colored with a dye. "A 'Winnipeg goldeye' represents the triumph of art over nature," write W. A. Kennedy and William M. Sprules. "Its characteristic color results from an aniline dye. Its characteristic taste is essentially that of oakwood smoke. Its texture has been improved by freezing. Its name is derived from a lake where it is no longer caught in appreciable quantities."[1]

Both species move into streams to spawn. Goldeye eggs are semi-buoyant but mooneye eggs have been reported to be covered with a gelatinous coat so that they resemble frogs' eggs. Some ichthyologists, however, have challenged this assertion; it is possible that those eggs were infected with fungus or bacteria.

---

1. W. A. Kennedy and W. M. Sprules, *Goldeye in Canada* (Ottawa: Fisheries Research Board of Canada, 1967), p. 35, quoted in William Beverley Scott and Edwin J. Crossman, *Freshwater Fishes of Canada* (Ottawa: Fisheries Research Board of Canada, 1973), p. 331.

Freshwater Eels
(Family Anguillidae)

Eels, as everyone knows, have elongate, snakelike bodies. Their dorsal and anal fins have many rays, and both are joined by membrane to the tail fin. Eels have no pelvic fins, but the pectoral fins are well developed. They have small eyes, the lower jaw projects beyond the upper, and the anterior nostrils are at the ends of short tubes. Freshwater eels do have scales but they are deeply embedded in the skin. The scales do not overlap and are arranged in a herringbone pattern.

The American eel, *Anguilla rostrata.*

Eels have a distinctive type of larva, called a leptocephalus, which is ribbon-shaped and extremely transparent. Alive, they look like clear noodles; in the water only the pigment in their eyes gives them away. The tarpon and bonefish so prized by deep-sea fishers have similar larvae, and for that reason they are considered to be closely related to the eels.

American eels spawn in the sea, then move to fresh water for most of their lives. When they become sexually mature they return to the ocean, where they spawn and die. No one has actually witnessed the complete life cycle, but it has been pieced together from bits of information. First of all, the leptocephalus larvae are distinctive. They are found throughout much of the North Atlantic, the smallest in the area called the Sargasso Sea, southeast of Bermuda. Nearer the coast the larvae are larger, and along the coast we find transforming stages, called glass eels and, later, elvers. Most male eels, which tend to be smaller than females, remain along the coast; females tend to move far upstream, some even reaching the upper Great Lakes. After some years in fresh water, as the eels start to reach sexual maturity, their color changes from yellow olive to silvery and their eyes get larger. They move downstream and out to sea, where we lose track of them. One of the few records of eels in deep water is a photograph taken from a submersible research vessel in the Tongue of the Ocean, in the Bahamas. We still do not know exactly where or at what depth they spawn, what kind of courtship they have, how they find their mates, or any other details of their reproduction.

For a while there was even some question as to whether the American and European eels might be the same species. It was suggested that the major difference between them, the number of vertebrae, might simply be due to the length of time they spend as larvae before reaching their respective coasts. But both kinds of larvae seem to be present near Iceland, and it is now generally accepted that they are different, though very similar, species.

Do not confuse eels with lampreys. Eels are true bony fishes, with well-developed jaws and a single pair of gill openings. Unlike lampreys, which have no paired fins, the American eel has well-developed pectoral fins. Some marine eels, such as the morays, have secondarily lost their pectoral fins.

Herrings and Shads
(Family Clupeidae)

Herrings are compressed silvery fishes with a row of sharp scales along the ventral edge of the abdomen, minute teeth, abdominal pelvic fins, a single dorsal fin, and a forked tail. They have no fin spines, no adipose fin, and no lateral line on the body, although their head canals have many branches. Some species, usually called shads, are anadromous, spending most of their lives in the ocean

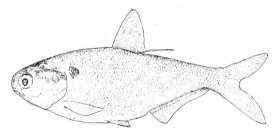

The gizzard shad, *Dorosoma cepedianum*.

but returning to fresh water to spawn. In the eastern United States, about five species are anadromous; the alewife has both anadromous and landlocked populations.

Most herrings live in temperate seas. They generally travel in schools, and their abundance and oily flesh make them an extremely important source of fish oils and protein for food and fertilizer.

Some herrings, however, spend their entire lives in fresh water. In the eastern United States, the gizzard shad and the threadfin shad are freshwater species that occasionally stray into brackish or salt water. In both species the last ray of the dorsal fin is elongated into a filament, and the young have a prominent shoulder spot partly surrounded by a white ring; it fades as they grow. When these species live in turbid waters, schools of semitransparent young swimming near the surface look like holes in water the color of coffee with cream.

Gizzard shads get their name from a muscular stomach that resembles the gizzard of a fowl. They also have special sacs at the tops of the gill arches, called epibranchial organs. Plankton strained from the water by the gill rakers is swept into the epibranchial organs and stored there for a time before being swallowed.

Sometimes in the spring you will come across the remains of large herrings washed up on shore. Hold your breath and take a good look at the bones that form the serrate edge of the belly. When you find a specimen in the right stage of decomposition, you will see that these are more than simple scales. Each one has a long bony strut extending well up the side within the body wall.

Alewives and other river shads have terminal mouths and lack the extended dorsal fin ray. They may have one or more shoulder spots. They do not have epibranchial organs or gizzards.

The largest of the river shads is the American shad; in fact, it is one of the largest herrings in the world, sometimes reaching a weight of 14 pounds. It is one of the most important commercial fishes on the Atlantic coast and it has been established on the Pacific coast as well. Shad season in the Hudson River runs from March 15 to late May or early June. The migrating shad are caught in gill nets set on poles or anchored in the lower river but allowed to drift with the tide farther upstream. Shad are valued most for their roe, but the flesh is also very good if you can master the special technique required to remove the bones. Other river shads are the Alabama shad, the hickory shad, the blueback herring, and the alewife. The skipjack herring lives in fresh waters of the Mississippi drainage.

In the story of the alewife in the Great Lakes we get a fascinating glimpse of the way people have changed natural communities. Before the arrival of Europeans, the Great Lakes had nicely balanced populations of small, medium-sized, and large fishes. In the deeper parts of the lakes the dominant predators were Atlantic salmon (Lake Ontario), lake trout, and burbot. Several species of ciscos and whitefish were present. Alewives probably entered Lake Ontario through the Erie Canal, which opened about 1825, although there is some reason to suspect that they were present in small numbers before the canal was built. As overfishing and loss of spawning grounds reduced the predators' populations, the alewives became extremely abundant. They competed so successfully with the plankton-eating whitefish and ciscos that some species became rare and then extinct. The pattern was repeated in the upper Great Lakes, which the alewives reached through the Welland Canal (a bypass around Niagara Falls). As the predators declined, the alewives increased and overwhelmed the native plankton eaters. The abundance of the alewives stimulated an increase in some minor predators, but then they, too, declined, and finally the deep-water planktivores were affected. The sea lamprey also moved into the upper Great Lakes through the Welland Canal and hastened the collapse of the large predators.

Apparently alewives are not completely adapted to life in fresh water. They are still very sensitive to thermal shock, and often in the spring when the tributaries warm faster than the deeper waters of the lakes, a line of dead alewives marks the boundary between warm and cold water. In the 1960s the carcasses of dead alewives formed huge windrows on the beaches of some lakes and clogged the screens of water intakes at power plants. This problem has subsided since Pacific salmon have become abundant in the Great Lakes.

Bullhead Catfishes
(Family Ictaluridae)

There are about thirty families of catfishes in the world but only one of them, the Ictaluridae, is native to North American fresh waters. Ictalurid catfishes are distinguished by four pairs of barbels on the head and an adipose dorsal fin. They have no scales and no true fin spines, although there are sharp, hard bony rays at the front of the dorsal and pectoral fins. The pelvic fins are abdominal.

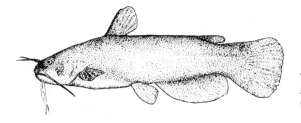

The yellow bullhead, *Ameiurus natalis*. Note the white chin barbels and the long anal fin.

Somehow, catfishes seem to have more personality than most other fishes. Perhaps it is because of their distinctive appearance, with their clean scaleless skin and long whisker-like barbels on the head. Perhaps it is their size; several species grow to 10 pounds and some North American species can reach more than 100 pounds. To me it is their lifestyle that makes them really interesting.

Bullhead catfishes fall into two groups. One, with flaglike adipose fins, includes the larger species, the bullheads, channel catfish, blue catfish, and flathead catfish. The other group comprises the madtoms, which are small, are often strikingly marked, and have keel-like adipose fins. Two species of blind catfish, *Satan eurystomus* and *Trogloglanis pattersoni*, are known from caves and wells near San Antonio, Texas.

Catfishes and bullheads tend to be rather secretive, keeping to deeper water or dense shelter most of the time. Some farm ponds contain large numbers of bullheads of which the owner is completely unaware. In the spring and early summer, however, you can often see clouds of tiny jet-black bullheads being herded by their parents in shallow water. From the shore the school looks like a black cloud that constantly changes shape as it moves along in the water. As the young grow, the schools break up and the young disperse into deeper water. Sometimes you will find solitary strays along the shore in water only a few inches deep. Presumably these individuals soon pay for their nonconformity by falling prey to birds and other terrestrial predators.

Catfishes lay rather large adhesive eggs that stick together in a rounded mass shaped like a thick pancake. The parents clean out a sheltered nest site under a rock or a log and guard the eggs, fanning them frequently so that the closely packed eggs do not suffocate. After the young hatch, the parents continue to guard them until they get to be an inch or more long. If you walk or snorkel along shorelines and weedy shallows in late spring and summer you may be able to locate nests and watch parents guarding them.

Sea catfishes of the family Ariidae live in salt water along our Atlantic and Gulf coasts. These catfishes, which have six instead of eight barbels, carry their eggs and young in their mouths. Their eggs are relatively huge, more than half an inch in diameter.

Catfishes feed near the bottom on invertebrates and organic matter. As their eyesight is rather weak, they depend principally on the chemical senses of taste and smell to find their food. Their barbels are richly supplied with taste buds, and catfishes constantly probe their environment with them.

Most madtoms are stream fishes. You can see them in rocky areas as you wade with a view box, especially at night. Some species that live in dense weed beds can be taken in a dip net or small seine. If you collect them, you should be aware that a poison gland associated with their pectoral fin spines can give a splendid sting.

In recent years an Asiatic clariid catfish has become established in Florida. Members of this family lack the adipose dorsal fin but they still manage to look like catfish. Because of their ability to breathe atmospheric air through a special chamber off their gill cavity, they are called walking catfish, and on wet nights they actually do wriggle overland to seek new habitats.

Suckers
(Family Catostomidae)

Suckers are related to the catfishes and share with them the presence of a Weberian apparatus, a set of structures that connect the air bladder to the ear. They have no teeth in the mouth but they do have a set of comblike pharyngeal teeth in the throat, behind the gills. These soft-rayed fish with no adipose fin have cycloid scales and abdominal pelvic fins. The tail is forked and the anal fin is set well back on the body. Most species have inferior, sucker-like mouths with thick lips.

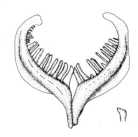

Pharyngeal arches of the white sucker, *Catostomus commersoni.*

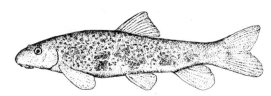

The streamlined longnose sucker, *Catostomus catostomus,* is nearly round in cross section. Its range includes eastern Siberia as well as much of North America.

Suckers get their name from their mouths, which are specialized for slurping up the organisms and detritus that make up their diet. They have thick rubbery lips and the mouth is positioned more or less on the underside of the head, usually behind the bulbous snout.

Southeast Asia has one species of sucker and the longnose sucker ranges into eastern Siberia, but all the rest live in North America.

Suckers strongly resemble minnows, and in fact the mouths of some minnows are very similar to those of suckers. They differ from minnows in the structure of the Weberian apparatus, and their pharyngeal teeth are more numerous and always in one row. These internal features, unfortunately, are of little help to the fish watcher.

The most useful characteristics are probably the mouth and the position of the anal fin, which is farther back in suckers than in minnows. (The distance from the beginning of the anal fin to the center of the base of the tail is about one-fifth of the fish's length in suckers, closer to one-third in minnows.)

The most abundant species in the northeast is the white sucker *Catostomus commersoni.* It is adaptable to a wide range of environmental conditions and lives in a correspondingly wide range of habitats. Apparently, however, it is not able to tolerate low pH; it has been hit hard by acid rain and has become much less abundant on the western slopes of the Adirondacks, where the effects of acid rain have been severe.

Suckers are famous for their spawning runs. Early in the spring they move into small creeks to spawn. At this time their colors intensify and they develop breeding tubercles, small horny points in the skin that help the fish to maintain contact during the spawning act. Usually they spawn over gravel bars, often in quite shallow water. For this reason suckers are a delight for the dry-land fish watcher. Take up a position on a high bank, or better, on a bridge, where you can get a good view of the spawning riffle. The males mill around in the spawning area while the females congregate in a pool just downstream. When a female is ready to spawn, she swims upstream and is flanked by two or more males. Then they all continue to swim upstream, vibrating and thrashing as they release the eggs and milt. The fertilized eggs drop to the bottom and lodge in the gravel. At the end of the run the female turns and swims back to the pool where she stays until she is ready to spawn again. The details of spawning vary, but the process is pretty much the same for all of the species that have been examined so far.

Some suckers live in rather swift waters. The hog sucker, *Hypentelium nigricans,* is often seen over rocky bottom in areas where the water is only a few inches deep. The top of the hog sucker's head is concave between its rather small eyes—a characteristic that is believed to be an advantage, perhaps enabling it to maintain its position near the bottom in swift water.

There are two main groups of North American suckers. One

group includes the large-scaled buffalo fishes, which have long dorsal fins supported by more than fourteen rays. The carpsuckers and the graceful blue sucker of the Mississippi-Missouri valley also belong to this group. All of the rest of the suckers have dorsal fins with fewer than fourteen rays.

The redhorses are especially colorful suckers with large scales. Except during the spawning season, they live in deeper parts of larger streams and are seldom seen. Sometimes they spawn in streams little wider than their own length.

Minnows
(Family Cyprinidae)

Although the term "minnow" is often applied to any small fish, in its technical sense it is reserved for members of the family Cyprinidae. With more than 230 species, this is the largest family of fishes in North America, and to my way of thinking it is the most interesting. Most minnows are small, some are tiny, and a few are huge. The Colorado squawfish, *Ptychochilus grandis*, can approach 6 feet in length. The introduced common carp and goldfish are minnows. In fact, throughout the world the family is known as the carp family.

Minnows are closely related to suckers, but their anal fins are

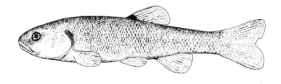

The creek chub, *Semotilus atromaculatus*, is one of the most widely distributed fishes in North America.

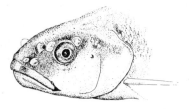

Nuptial tubercles on the head of a breeding male creek chub.

farther forward (the caudal peduncle is longer) and their pharyngeal teeth are quite different (one, two, or three rows with five or fewer teeth in the main row and only one or two teeth, if any, in the lesser row). Common carp and goldfish have three rows of teeth on each bone; native minnows have only one or two. Neither minnows nor suckers have teeth on the bones of their jaws. Most minnows have terminal mouths, whereas most suckers have inferior, sucker-like mouths.

Native North American minnows have fewer than eight soft rays in the dorsal fin, but the introduced common carp and goldfish have long fins with more than twenty rays. Carp and goldfish also have hard, serrated spines at the front of the dorsal and anal fins. Minnows dominate the fresh waters of North America, Eurasia, and Africa but they are absent from South America and Australia.

From the observer's point of view, minnows can be identified as dace, which are small with very fine scales; shiners, which are predominantly silvery; and chubs, which are stout-bodied and less silvery. Anything else is just a minnow. These are informal categories and their only real use is to help us remember what we see in the field.

Minnows do all their chewing with their pharyngeal teeth, which are on two bones just behind the gills. These bones are, in fact, modified gill arches. The structure of the pharyngeal teeth is related to the fish's diet. Herbivores tend to have flat grinding surfaces on the individual teeth; carnivores have various hooks and cutting edges.

Despite their lack of jaw teeth, minnows exhibit a remarkable array of feeding habits. Species that feed in mid-water tend to have terminal mouths—that is, the opening of the mouth is at the very front of the fish. Those that feed at the surface have mouths that are directed upward, and those that feed on the bottom have the mouth on the underside of the snout. (We use the terms "terminal," "superior," and "inferior" in this case to indicate position, not quality.) The stoneroller minnow makes its living by scraping diatoms and other organisms off rocks. Its lower jaw has a cartilaginous rim that is perfectly suited for this task.

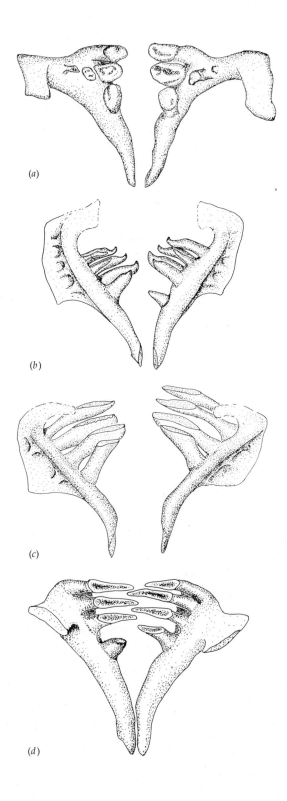

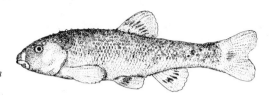

The stoneroller minnow, *Campostoma anomalum*.

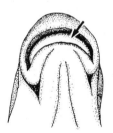

The stoneroller uses the cartilaginous ridge on its lower jaw to scrape diatoms from rocks.

One of the more unlikely methods of feeding is that of the cutlips minnow, *Exoglossum maxillingua*. Its extremely specialized lower jaw has a central bony blade surmounted on each side by a fleshy lobe. With this blade the cutlips can remove the eye of another fish in a fraction of a second. The cutlips probably does not normally feed on the eyes of other fishes, but anglers know that fishes crowded into the same bait pail with a cutlips minnow frequently end up with one eye missing.

Minnows' breeding habits are diverse and fascinating. During the breeding season the males of many species develop special colors—bright red, yellow, green, steel blue. Some develop bright red or iridescent yellow fins. They also develop breeding tubercles in a pattern that is distinct for each species. In some species these tubercles are so minute that they are visible only under magnification.

Dorsal views of the pharyngeal teeth of minnows, anterior ends at the bottom. (*a*) The common carp, *Cyprinus carpio*, has three rows of pharyngeal teeth on each side, with a single tooth in each of the outer rows and three in the inner rows. (*b*) The creek chub, *Semotilus atromaculatus*, is a carnivorous species with pointed and hooked teeth. The tooth formula is 2, 5–4, 2. One tooth is missing from the inner row on the left side. (*c*) The stoneroller, *Campostoma anomalum*, has a single row of four teeth on each side. In this species the teeth have grinding surfaces. Note the crenulated edge on the third tooth at the left. (*d*) The bluntnose minnow, *Pimephales notatus*, is another herbivorous species with a grinding surface on each tooth.

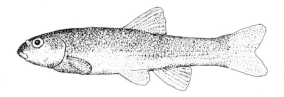

The cutlips minnow, *Exoglossum maxillingua*.

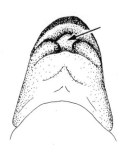

The cutlips minnow sometimes uses the hard, bladelike central lobe of its lower jaw to remove the eyes of other fishes for a snack.

Such tiny tubercles give the skin a sandpaper-like roughness. The few large tubercles on the head of the creek chub are so conspicuous that they have earned the species its alternative name, horned dace. Bluntnose minnow males have a moustache of very large tubercles on the tip of the snout, and similar patterns occur in their near relatives, including the fathead minnow and the bullhead minnow. Ichthyologists find tubercle patterns useful as indications of relationships, and the fish themselves probably use them to identify their mates and competitors.

Some minnows are nest builders. If you walk along a stream bank in the spring you are likely to see places that look as if someone had dumped a wheelbarrow load of gravel into the stream. These are nests that the males have built by picking up stones in their mouths and carrying them to the chosen site, one by one. Several species of chubs build such nests, which can be several feet in diameter. When the fish spawn over the pile, the eggs fall into crevices between the stones and are thus protected from being eaten by other fishes, or even by the parents themselves.

The fathead minnow, *Pimephales promelas*, uses a different approach. The male selects and cleans a spot on the underside of some structure, such as a log or a large stone. He then courts a female, who deposits a single layer of eggs on the roof of the nest cavity. The male guards the nest against all comers, and he periodically rubs the eggs with the thick fatty pad in front of his dorsal fin (this is where the species gets its name) to keep them clear of silt so they can respire.

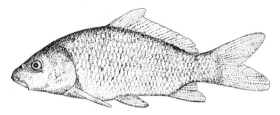

The common carp, *Cyprinus carpio.*

There is no denying that some species of minnows are difficult to identify. Difficult but not impossible. Some species require close examination under a microscope, but most species have features of structure or behavior that enable a patient observer to identify them even from the shore.

Michigan

June 18, 1980. Wilderness State Park, Michigan. 2 P.M. We are standing on a beach on the Lower Peninsula side of the Straits of Mackinac, where lakes Huron and Michigan come together. To our right we can see the great bridge that connects the Upper and Lower peninsulas, the graceful curves of its suspension cables glistening in the sunlight. The beach before us is gravel and coarse sand, boasting of the violence of the winter storms that sweep this region. Around the point to our left is a shallow weedy area that is justly famed as one of the best smallmouth bass fishing areas in the Midwest, but today our attention is focused on a long chain of partly connected pools that parallels the beach, separated from the pale-blue straits by a rampart of sand and gravel. From our vantage point we can see that the pools extend to the east a quarter of a mile or more.

The pools are not very old. Most of them are less than 30 feet wide and less than 3 feet deep, with patches of spindly bulrushes and a bottom of flocculent gray and yellow marl over sand. An incongruous cement boat-launching ramp leads into the pool directly in front of us. It must have been built for access to the straits, but it is now more than 100 feet from the actual shoreline. The barrier beach rampart stands like a spite fence as a tangible warning to those who would presume to trespass against mighty Lake Michigan.

As we look down into the slightly brownish water, a fluttery movement catches our eye. Soon a dark reddish fish about 2 inches long rushes forward about four feet, then suddenly stops, turns, and swims slowly back toward a beer can that is partially sunken in the bottom. A few seconds later he again rushes forward, stops, and leisurely returns to the can. Now we understand that he is defending the territory around the can, and that his rushes are chases as he drives off less conspicuous fish that he sees as threats to his nest. In a few minutes he disappears into one of the triangular openings in the can. My companion removes his shoes and socks, wades out, and retrieves the can. As he pours the contents into my hand, the fish flops out. It is a male fathead minnow, dark gray with lighter bands and a yellowish cast on the lower sides. Overall it is suffused with a coppery hue that gives it a reddish tone in the water. An irregular black band crosses the lower part of its dorsal fin, and across its upper lip a double row of large horny points juts out like an overwaxed moustache. On its back, behind the head and in front of the dorsal fin, is a wide ridge of swollen fatty tissue.

The beer can is the modernistic nest of this male. Earlier a female, or perhaps more than one, plastered a hundred or more eggs on the inside roof of the can. Between chases the male returns to the can to care for the developing eggs, caressing them with his dorsal pad.

Gently we release the male and carefully return the can to its resting place, in the position in which we found it. In a few minutes the male returns and resumes guarding the nest and its eggs as if nothing had happened.

A few days later we again visit the pools, this time with a class of fish students. Carefully we wade some of the pools, and in an hour we find three other nests under pieces of wood. We see other males defending territories but can't seem to spot their nests. Nearby, schools of female fatheads with dark stripes along their sides go about their daily tasks. Their role in the reproductive process is over.

Characins
(Family Characidae)

The characins are fishes of tropical Africa and Central and South America. Only one species, the Mexican tetra, gets into the southern United States. Our species has a deep, compressed, silvery body, a forked tail, and a small adipose dorsal fin. Characins are ostariophysans, but unlike suckers and minnows, they have strong teeth in the mouth. The South American piranhas and the African tigerfishes are characins.

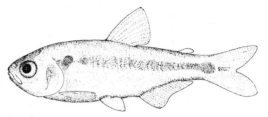

The Mexican tetra, *Astyanax mexicanus.*

At first glance *Astyanax mexicanus,* the Mexican tetra, might be mistaken for some kind of herring because of its deep, compressed, silvery body and the dusky spots on the upper side behind the head. Its strong teeth and adipose dorsal fin, however, soon lay that impression to rest. The tetra is more colorful than a herring and has a black line on the caudal peduncle, extending on to the tail. Some individuals have yellow and red pigment on the tail and lower fins.

Originally the Mexican tetra lived as far north as southern Texas and New Mexico, but it has since been introduced into several other southern states as well as areas of Texas where it did not occur naturally.

Aquarists will immediately recognize this rather colorful species as a relative of some of their familiar pets. It is closely related to the blind cave tetra of Mexico.

Trouts and Salmons
(Family Salmonidae)

Trouts and salmons are graceful, robust fishes with a well-developed adipose dorsal fin, no true fin spines, and abdominal

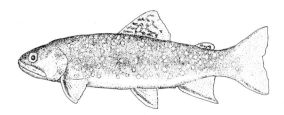

The brook trout, *Salvelinus fontinalis.*

pelvic fins. The family includes whitefishes, which are silvery-white lake-dwelling species, graylings, trouts, chars, and salmons. There are about forty species in North America, including the introduced brown trout. Salmonids also live in Eurasia and in the Atlas Mountains of North Africa.

Trouts

There is a little problem with the terms "trout" and "salmon." In general, trout are stream fishes and salmons are anadromous—they spend most of their lives in the ocean but swim into streams to spawn. There are landlocked populations of salmons, however, and sea-run strains of trouts. The problem becomes even more interesting when we consider the relationships of the trouts and salmons: the rainbow and cutthroat trouts are salmons and the Atlantic salmon is a trout. Furthermore, the fine-scaled char are trouts, but there are pronounced differences between them and the ordinary trouts.

In the cold waters of the Northeast, the trouts are the premier sport fishes. For many anglers other fish simply do not exist. Four species are native to the northeastern states: the Atlantic salmon, the lake trout, the brook trout, and farther north in New England and Canada the arctic char. The other well-known species were introduced, the brown trout from Europe and the rainbow from the western United States. Brook, brown, and rainbow trouts are stream fishes, easily seen from shore. Salmon and lake trout live in deep water and the only ones you are likely to see are those in a fisher's creel. Some lake trout spawn in water less than 10 feet deep, but they pick November to do so, when conditions are less than ideal for fish watching.

Young trout of all species have vertical bars called parr marks on their sides. Adult trouts are easily distinguishable, but the young can be quite hard to tell apart when they are less than 2 inches long. The brook trout is a dark fish with worm-shaped marks on its upper sides and back and pale spots. Its lower fins have brilliant white leading edges. Brook trout and lake trout belong to the group called char, distinguished by their very small scales. Lake trout are more streamlined than brook trout and have deeply forked tails.

Brown trout have dark spots on a lighter background, but the spots are scarce or not present on the tail. Many of the brown trout's spots have light halos. Brown trout have red spots on the sides. Rainbows also have small dark spots on a paler background over the back and upper sides, and these spots are present on the upper half of the tail. Rainbows have no red spots but large rainbows have a red band along the side. Recently it was established that rainbows and the western cutthroat trout are actually closely related to the Pacific salmons, so these species, along with the Apache trout and the golden trout, had to be transferred from the genus *Salmo* to the genus *Oncorhynchus*. Furthermore, for technical reasons the scientific name of the species of the rainbow had to be changed from *gairdneri* to *mykiss*, so it is now known as *Oncorhynchus mykiss* rather than *Salmo gairdneri*.

The Catskills, October 31, 1980

Comma-shaped Crystal Lake in Sullivan County, in the hills south of Roscoe, New York, is a real prize. Its shores were once the sites of private estates. Later, as state land, it was leased to a summer camp, and now, with only the dam and a few building foundations to remind us of its place in human history, it is managed as a special trout fishing lake. In 1975 the existing fish populations were removed and the lake was restocked with brook trout.

We have picked a near-perfect day with only a few puffy clouds and the temperature sneaking into the high 50s. Our only complaint is a gusty wind that ruffles the water's surface and makes it difficult to keep our canoe in one place.

Brook trout that spawn in lakes choose areas where there are upwell-ings from underwater springs. Such areas are usually offshore from valleys where streams flow into the lake. We paddle toward the north-ern part of the lake, hoping to find spawning brook trout to photo-graph.

Near the outlet where we launched our canoe, the water was soupy green, the result of planktonic algae in water that was pushed toward the dam, but in the open lake the algae are sparse, drifting like green dust in the clear water. We ease our canoe in toward shore until we can see the bottom 6 feet or so below. As we follow the edge of a narrow shelf, our course takes us within 15 to 30 feet of the forested shoreline.

A few days ago the hills must have been a blaze of color but now the leaves have fallen and the slopes are silvery gray, punctuated by clumps of dark-green conifers. At the water's edge a few shrubs retain their brightly colored leaves. We decide that they must be ornamentals left from estate days.

As we glide along we pay careful attention to submerged logs and rocks, hoping to catch a glimpse of trout. For a time we see nothing. Then, as we pass a submerged brush pile close to the shore, a school of small fish flash by. They pass too quickly for a good look, but my guess is golden shiners.

Suddenly my companion at the bow paddle sees a trout, then anoth-er, and as we stop paddling, the canoe drifts over a pale-yellow area on the bottom, some 6 feet in diameter. A canoe length away we see a slightly smaller cleared area. As we reverse our strokes to bring the canoe over the light spots, the wake momentarily smoothes the surface and we see a group of foot-long trout milling about over clean yellow-ish bottom. The brilliant white edges of their lower fins leave no doubt that we have found the spawning redds, or nests, of the brook trout. They do not seem to be disturbed by our canoe.

Even with our Polaroid glasses, the wind-ruffled surface makes it difficult to see, and photographing through the surface is out of the question, so we decide to continue around the lake to other redds in areas that are out of the wind. At the head of the lake we pass a group of smaller trout, apparently spooked by our approach, but we see no more redds.

Back at the parking lot I load the underwater camera with high-speed film while Marjie finds a rock that will serve as an anchor and gathers all the line we have, including the tie-downs from the canoe rack. *As we paddle back to the redds I ponder the camera settings. With the water, the low sun angle, and the dark background, I decide to use f8 and f16 at 1/125 second.*

At the redds we try to judge the wind, and at what seems to be a reasonable distance Marjie eases our makeshift anchor to the bottom while I turn to face the stern of the canoe with camera and view box ready. At first the canoe comes to rest some 25 feet from the redds, but on the second try it is close enough so that we can see both redds as the canoe swings to its anchor.

Through the view box the pale areas we saw from the surface are revealed as gravel that has been swept clean. In their spawning livery the sexes are easily distinguished. The females are paler with conspicuous light spots on their sides. The darker males have brilliant red lower flanks. The brightly colored males greatly outnumber the females; we see only three or four females but at least fifteen males. The females appear to be about 10 inches long, the males a little larger. One male appears to be shorter than the others; possibly he suffers from the curved spine sometimes seen in hatchery trout. Still he is as active and as brilliantly colored as the rest of the males.

I push the underwater camera through the surface and start shooting. All I can see through the surface is a blur, so I aim blindly and hope for the best. When the film in the Nikonos gives out, I try the other camera through the view box, but there are so many reflections that I soon give up. Photography finished, we turn the canoe end for end so Marjie can watch the spawners.

Inshore from the redds are many newts. Now and then one swims to the surface for a quick gulp of air. Once Marjie sees a slender form swim into view, then quickly rebury itself in the leaves that cover the bottom. Apparently a small eel has made its way up from the Delaware River. As the canoe passes over the redds one last time, Marjie is lucky enough to see a male position himself over a female and quiver briefly. Probably she has seen the actual spawning act.

Salmons

Atlantic salmon are sea fish that move into rivers to spawn, although there are also some landlocked populations. They tend to be silvery fish with X-shaped markings. They have short pectoral fins and a more deeply forked tail than the brown trout, but otherwise

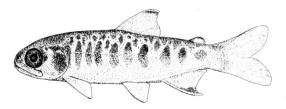

A juvenile coho salmon, *Oncorhynchus kisutch*.

the two species resemble each other. They are, in fact, closely related.

Pacific salmon are quite different, with a long anal fin that has thirteen or more rays. (Rainbows and cutthroats have short anal fins but share certain skeletal and life history features with the other Pacific salmons). Originally the Pacific salmons were found only in Pacific Coast streams, where they had returned from the sea to spawn. Some sockeye populations, however, are landlocked. In the last few years, several species have been successfully stocked in the Great Lakes, where they provide excellent and dramatic fishing. Four of the five American species—coho, chinook, pink, and kokanee (the landlocked form of the sockeye)—are now present and reproducing in at least a few tributaries of the Great Lakes.

One of the most dramatic sights anywhere is the spawning run of the Pacific salmon. In their native streams some species may travel as much as 1,000 miles inland to spawn. Large fish fight their way over waterfalls and through shallows until they reach their home gravel bars, where they spawn and die. Similar runs now occur in the Great Lakes. A trip to the salmon hatchery at Altmar, New York, in October is an unforgettable experience. The hatchery is located on a small tributary of the Salmon River, a few miles east of Lake Ontario, and the salmon come upstream from the lake by the thousands. Salmon that swim up a fish ladder become brood stock. The eggs are taken and fertilized, then the young are raised in the hatchery for later stocking. During the spawning run every little pool is filled with returning salmon, and every few seconds there is a great commotion as the 2-foot-long fish force their way over shallow riffles with their dorsal fins out of the water. Don't miss it.

Whitefishes and Ciscos

The salmon family also includes the whitefishes, the lake herrings, and their allies, the ciscos, which are sometimes sold as chubs (not to be confused with the minnows [cyprinids] that are called chubs). These deep-water fishes are ordinarily not seen by the fish watcher, though you can sometimes find juvenile lake whitefish in the shallows of the upper Great Lakes.

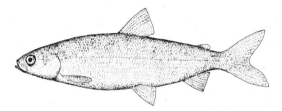

The lake herring, *Coregonus artedi.*

Smelts
(Family Osmeridae)

Smelts are rather small, slender, torpedo-shaped fishes, silvery with rough scales and a well-developed adipose fin. Smelts have prominent teeth, including large fangs on the tip of the tongue. The rainbow smelt lives in the fresh waters of the eastern United States and has both freshwater and anadromous populations. It was introduced into the upper Great Lakes drainage, probably in 1912. There is a debate as to whether these smelts made their way to Lake Ontario through natural streams or through canals. A second northeastern species, the pygmy smelt, lives in deep lakes in eastern Canada and New England.

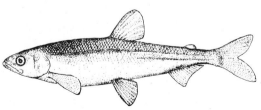

The rainbow smelt, *Osmerus mordax.*
Notice the small adipose dorsal fin
behind the regular dorsal fin.

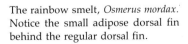

At first glance the rainbow smelt, *Osmerus mordax*, looks a little like a slender minnow, but a close look reveals strong teeth on the jaws and tongue and a small adipose dorsal fin. Its scales are rough.

During most of the year smelts live in water too deep to be readily seen by the fish watcher. In the spring, however, they move into streams to spawn at night, and in many areas people are permitted to take a certain number of them in dip nets. During the day they drop back to the lake until the next night. They make an excellent meal and there is a commercial fishery for them in some of the Great Lakes. Commercial fishers catch them in trawls. Sometimes the young of the year are caught in small seines near the shore. They are quite elongate and transparent until they are about 2 inches long. Anadromous smelts run into small coastal streams.

Pikes and Pickerels
(Family Esocidae)

Pikes and pickerels are elongate, barracuda-shaped fishes with broad, flattened, elongate jaws with prominent teeth. Their dorsal and anal fins are set far back and the tail is forked. Pikes and pickerels have no adipose fins and no fin spines. Their scales are smooth and their colors include greenish or brownish tones to match their weedy habitat.

The redfin pickerel, *Esox americanus americanus*.

The arrow-shaped esocids are extremely effective predators—sort of the freshwater counterpart of the barracudas, though the families are not related. All esocid fishes are well camouflaged, capable of quick bursts of speed, and have large mouths with formidable, sharply pointed teeth, so they have no trouble taking care of their prey once they have caught it. Their long, flattened jaws have been described as looking like a duck's bill, but no duck has teeth like a pike.

The family is small. Four species are native to North America; one of them, the northern pike, also lives in Europe. Another species that lives in Siberia has been introduced in a few places in North America.

The smallest species are the grass and redfin pickerels, which reach 14 to 16 inches; the largest, the muskellunge, probably can attain weights close to 100 pounds. Northern pike reach nearly 50 pounds and the chain pickerel about 10.

Northern pike, chain pickerel, and muskellunge are northern species that live in lakes and the slower parts of large rivers, where their preferred habitat is weedy shallows. The redfin and grass pickerels, too, live in weedy areas. They can often be seen hovering almost motionless near the surface, waiting for they prey.

The redfin and grass pickerel occur in a ring around the Appalachian highlands. The grass pickerel, *Esox americanus vermiculatus*, lives on the western slopes and the redfin pickerel, *Esox americanus americanus*, lives on the eastern side. At the northern limit of their range, in the St. Lawrence drainage, they live together in a few places but apparently do not interbreed. Along the Gulf Coast, however, the populations are intermediate and vary slightly from stream drainage to stream drainage. Since these populations cannot be definitely assigned to the eastern or the western form, we call them intergrades and consider the redfin and grass pickerels to be subspecies.

Most pikes and pickerels have similar color patterns when they are small, so they can be quite difficult to distinguish. Juvenile muskellunge, however, are pale with dark spots along their sides and are quite distinctive.

Mudminnows
(Family Umbridae)

Mudminnows are small, brownish, cigar-butt shaped fish with short dorsal and anal fins set well back on the body. Their tails are rounded with a dark pigment bar at the base. They have no spines

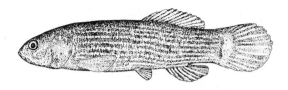

The eastern mudminnow, *Umbra pygmaea*.

and no adipose dorsal fin. The pelvic fins are abdominal, the scales are smooth, and the head is bullet-shaped.

Mudminnows are secretive fishes that live in weedy areas where there is a great deal of plant debris. They are not true minnows but relatives of the pikes and pickerels.

There are three species in the genus *Umbra*, two in eastern North America, one in Europe. The genus *Novumbra* consists of one species in the Olympic Peninsula of Washington. The two eastern species live in swamps and other densely vegetated areas. The family also includes the Alaskan blackfish, which is reputed to revive after being frozen in solid ice. This tale may well be true. As long as the fish itself does not freeze, it probably can withstand being immobilized when the water freezes around it.

The central mudminnow, *Umbra limi*, lives throughout much of the Midwest and as far east as the Hudson River. The eastern mudminnow, *Umbra pygmaea*, has a more restricted range on the East Coast. The central mudminnow has irregular bands on its body; the eastern mudminnow has quite distinct lines on its sides. Both species have a dark bar at the base of the tail.

Because they live in very shallow waters, mudminnows are often caught in dip nets. They can tolerate low oxygen and low temperatures and apparently burrow into soft muck and leaf debris during the winter.

The scientific name *Umbra* means shadow, which is an excellent description of these little swamp dwellers.

Pirate Perch
(Family Aphredoderidae)

The pirate perch is a strange little fish with a robust body, rather large mouth, and rough scales. It has no adipose dorsal fin but it

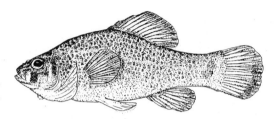

The heavy-bodied pirate perch, *Aphredoderus sayanus,* has its vent far forward, between the gill covers.

does have three or four true spines in the front of the dorsal and anal fins. There is only one living species, *Aphredoderus sayanus,* but fossils of other species are known.

You may not see them in the water, but pirate perches are such interesting little fishes that you should know something about them. In some ways the pirate perch is an anatomical absurdity. When it is young its anus is in the usual position, just in front of the anal fin, but as the fish grows, the anal and urogenital openings migrate forward until they are in the throat region, between the gill covers.

Why the forward vent? This anatomical specialization is found also in the American cavefishes of the family Amblyopsidae and the marine pearlfish, which lives in sea cucumbers. Can it be associated with life in a small hole? Does it have something to do with the fish's breeding habits? Or is it a specialization that has been passed along by heredity long after it has lost its original purpose?

The pirate perch's single dorsal fin has both spines and rays. The belly is only slightly lighter than the back, an indication that it spends most of its time concealed and out of bright sunlight. Its distribution is interesting, too. It lives in low-lying regions surrounding the Appalachian mountain chain, from the Lake Ontario drainage in western New York through the Ohio and Mississippi valleys and along the Gulf and Atlantic coasts north to Long Island. The Lake Ontario populations seem to be separated from the Mississippi Valley populations by a wide gap in Ohio and Pennsylvania.

Pirate perches live in weedy places in slow-moving streams. In life they are dark brown or yellowish brown with a slightly purplish cast. A dark bar at the base of the tail is similar to that seen in the mudminnows.

Trout-Perch
(Family Percopsidae)

The percopsids, another family of distinctive small fishes, are rather transparent in life with some blotches along the sides. The body tapers from a rather large head back to a forked tail. The prominent conical snout overhangs the mouth. Trout-perches have spines at the fronts of the dorsal and anal fins, and they also have an adipose dorsal fin, an unusual combination. One of the two species lives in the Pacific northwest; the other, *Percopsis omiscomaycus*, ranges from the Atlantic Coast to the Yukon drainage in Alaska. These small fishes seldom exceed 6 inches in total length.

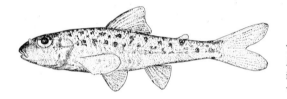

The small, translucent trout-perch, *Percopis omiscomaycus*, has a tiny adipose dorsal fin and a large head with a protuberant snout.

The trout-perch has a self-contradictory name for the very good reason that its anatomy is paradoxical. Only rather primitive teleosts have adipose dorsal fins and only advanced fish have true spines in the vertical fins, yet the trout-perch has both. Catfishes have fin spines and an adipose dorsal fin but their spines are modified soft rays, not true spines.

Trout-perch have an undershot jaw and a prominent, bluntly pointed snout. They also have large canals on the head. In life they are a transparent gray with rows of darker spots. Their maximum length is around 6 or 7 inches. In some waters they are abundant, but as far as I know, they are of no interest to anglers. They probably are important forage for larger fishes.

The other species of living trout-perch is the sand roller, *Percopsis transmontana*, from the Columbia River of Washington, Oregon, and Idaho. This distribution, somewhat similar to that of the mudminnows, is of considerable interest to biologists.

Trout-perch live in lakes and streams. They spawn at night in late spring and early summer, when they can be seen in shallow areas. The sticky eggs are scattered over the bottom and become covered with sand grains.

Burbot
(Family Gadidae)

Codfishes are extremely important to the world economy as a food source. Most are rather large marine fishes with high-quality flesh. Until recently they were so abundant that the sea seemed to be capable of feeding the world's population indefinitely, but during the last three or four decades this assumption has been shown to be false. With the decline of the Atlantic cod, the fishing fleets have turned to other species, only to find that they, too, are far from inexhaustible.

The burbot, *Lota lota,* ranges across Eurasia as well as all of northern North America. Notice the prominent single barbel at the tip of the lower jaw of this freshwater codfish.

Two codfishes venture into fresh waters in the Northeast. One is the little tomcod, *Microgadus tomcod,* which moves into northern estuaries to spawn in the dead of winter; the other is the freshwater burbot, *Lota lota.* The tomcod is an almost perfect miniature of the Atlantic cod, with three dorsal and two anal fins, but it never gets much more than a foot long. Even so, it makes a fair pan fish in estuaries such as the Hudson and in more northern rivers.

The burbot—sometimes called ling, lawyer, and several other local names—is an elongate fish with two dorsal fins, neither of which has spines. The first is short and the second very long. Its tail is paddle-shaped and its pelvic fins are quite far forward. A single prominent barbel adorns the tip of the lower jaw. Burbots have smooth, embedded scales and a slimy skin. The young are dark brown, sometimes almost black. Older fish have rather pretty mottled patterns.

Most burbots live in lakes, but there are a few stream populations. They are rather secretive and seldom seen. There is a stream population in the upper reaches of the Susquehanna River in New York State. The fish spend most of their time hiding under flat rocks. If one is disturbed, it moves to another hole so quickly that you wonder if you really saw it.

The burbot was one of the most abundant large predators in the Great Lakes. Fishers consider it inferior to other species. There are stories of ice fishers stacking burbot carcasses like cordwood to build windbreaks.

The burbot occurs all across Europe and northern Asia as well as throughout the northern part of North America.

Cavefishes
(Family Amblyopsidae)

The Amblyopsidae are a small family of cave- and spring-dwelling fishes in the Appalachian and Ozark regions, north to southern Indiana. They are soft-rayed fishes with no adipose dorsal fin and with small or no pelvic fins. Like the pirate perch, the cavefishes have the anal and urogenital openings far forward, between the gill covers. The eyes of species that live underground are reduced and nonfunctional, and the fish have lost most of their pigment, so that they appear white or pinkish. The species that live in surface waters, the swampfish and the spring cavefish, have pigment and small but functional eyes. There are about six species.

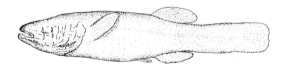

The northern cavefish, *Amblyopsis spelaea*, lacks eyes but it does have small pelvic fins.

If you visit some of the commercial caves in central Kentucky, you may be shown specimens or photographs of the northern cavefish, *Amblyopsis spelaea*. This is the only species of cavefish that has well-developed pelvic fins. The southern cavefish, *Typhlichthys subterraneus*, has a disjunct range. It occurs from southern Indiana to northwestern Georgia and also in the Ozark Plateau, west of the Mississippi River. Two other species, the Ozark cavefish and the Alabama cavefish, are considered to be endangered. The family contains two more species: the swampfish, *Chologaster cornuta*, of the Atlantic Coast, and the spring cavefish, *Forbesichthys agassizi*, of Illinois, Kentucky, Tennessee, and Missouri. The swampfish is a surface dweller with well-developed eyes and pigment; the spring cavefish is intermediate between it and the blind, unpigmented cavefishes. Keep in mind that there are blind catfishes that live underground as well.

Killifishes
(Family Cyprinodontidae)

Killifishes (sometimes called topminnows or toothed carps) are small, minnow-like fishes that tend to live near the surface. They have smooth scales, no adipose dorsal fin, scaly heads, and terminal or superior mouths. Most are rather colorful during the breeding season and have vertical bars or sometimes longitudinal stripes.

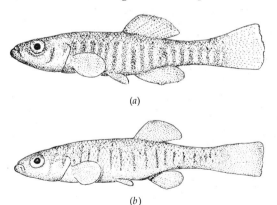

(*a*)

(*b*)

The male (*a*) and female (*b*) banded killifish, *Fundulus diaphanus*.

Killifishes are egg layers. The females have a membranous oviductal sheath around the front of the anal fin.

Killifishes are popular aquarium fishes. Some authorities divide the family into Cyprinodontidae (pupfishes) and Fundulidae (killifishes and topminnows); others place them all in a single family.

Because they are surface dwellers, killifishes are relatively easy to see even in turbid water. It is sometimes hard to get a good look at them, but they can often be identified by their habits.

Most killifishes are less than 4 inches long. Their dorsal and anal fins lack spines and are set relatively far back on the body. Their shape ranges from rather stout to quite slender. In life their colors range from gray-green to brownish and most species have some kind of vertical bars, although a few species have broad lateral stripes along the mid-sides. Males of some species are quite colorful. Characteristically the mouth is aimed upward. Pupfishes and their allies have short deep bodies; killifishes and topminnows are rather elongate.

Most cyprinodonts are restricted to the warmer parts of North America but a few range into southern Canada. A common euryhaline species along the Atlantic Coast is the mummichog, *Fundulus heteroclitus,* a rather stout species with a very short snout. Females have narrow vertical bars widely spaced; males have wider bars that are closer together and tend to become uniformly dark as they get larger. Breeding males are quite bluish with bright yellow underparts. They also have an ocellus (a black spot surrounded by a yellow ring) in the dorsal fin.

Mummichogs can often be seen in the shallows. One of their characteristic behaviors is to jump out of the water and skitter erratically along the surface when they are alarmed. As you guide your canoe into a tidal marsh, you may sometimes drive schools of mummichogs into the shallows. There, at the last moment, they go into their confusion behavior so that the water explodes with jumping fish. It certainly confuses the human observer and probably has a similar effect on wading birds and other natural predators.

The freshwater banded killifish, *Fundulus diaphanus,* lives in lakes and slow streams in the Northeast. This is a fish of weedy shallows.

Altogether there are fifty-three species of killifishes in the fresh waters of the United States and Canada.

A related and similar family called Rivulidae or Aplocheilidae is represented by one species, *Rivulus marmoratus,* in Florida and along the Gulf Coast. Its common name is mangrove rivulus and it lives in crab holes and similar shelter near the coast.

Livebearers
(Family Poeciliidae)

Closely related to the killifishes, male livebearers are easy to recognize because the anterior rays of the anal fins of the males are modified into a complex structure, the gonopodium, which is used to transfer sperm to the female's reproductive tract. Livebearers are small, even tiny fishes that have smooth scales, no fin spines, and no adipose dorsal fin. The have superior mouths, scaly heads, and abdominal pelvic fins. About twenty-one species live in North America.

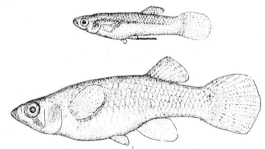

The western mosquitofish, *Gambusia affinis.*

Livebearers such as the guppy, mollies, and swordtails are familiar to most people because of their popularity as aquarium pets. Most of our native livebearers are confined to the warmer waters of the South, but the mosquitofish has cold-hardy populations as far north as Chicago and the same strain has been introduced on Long Island. It is a rather nondescript dull-gray species usually less than 2 inches long.

In the southern states gambusias and the colorful mollies are easy to see in bayous and borrow pits along the highways. Frequently you will be able to watch their courtship from shore.

In small ponds with no predators the mosquitofish will venture into open waters, but when predators are around it keeps close to shelter near shore.

Silversides
(Family Atherinidae)

Silversides are slender surface-dwelling fishes with a brilliant silver streak along their mid-sides. The family is mostly marine and includes the famous grunion of the California beaches. They have two well-separated dorsal fins, the first consisting of four slender spines, the second all soft rays.

In life the surface-dwelling brook silverside, *Labidesthes sicculus,* is greenish and nearly transparent, with a bright silvery mid-lateral stripe.

Like the marine flying fishes, to which they are distantly related, the silversides have superior mouths and their pectoral fins are high on their sides. The freshwater species are rather small but some marine representatives of this family are eaten as whitebait. Apart from their lateral silver stripe, these fishes are nearly transparent with a faint greenish or yellow cast, so that they are nearly invisible in the water.

The brook silverside, *Labidesthes sicculus,* is widespread in the eastern United States. It lives in lakes and slow streams around vegetation. The inland silverside, *Menidia beryllina,* ascends rivers and also has landlocked populations.

Sticklebacks
(Family Gasterosteidae)

Sticklebacks get their name from their dorsal spines, which are not connected by membranes, as such spines usually are. They are all

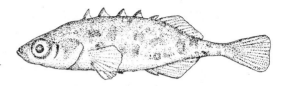

The brook stickleback, *Culaea incon-
stans*.

small fishes, the largest less than 5 inches long. Some of them live in
fresh water, some in salt water, some in both. Four species occur in
our area. Sticklebacks lack scales, although some populations of the
threespine sticklebacks have bony plates along the sides. The dorsal,
anal, and pelvic spines are locked in the erect position.

The tiny sticklebacks are truly distinctive fishes. They all have extremely slender caudal peduncles and a tiny upturned mouth, often
at the end of a rather tubular face.

Sticklebacks are generally named according to the number of their
dorsal spines: threespine, fourspine, ninespine, and brook sticklebacks occur in our area. The fourspine is a coastal species that lives
in estuaries, the brook stickleback is strictly a freshwater species,
and the threespine and ninespine have both freshwater and marine
populations. Most sticklebacks live in shallow water, but the ninespine lives in deep lakes as well.

Sticklebacks are perhaps best known for their mating and nesting
habits. Nikolaas Tinbergen's studies of their elaborate courtship rituals helped to win him a Nobel prize. The male builds a barrel-
shaped nest of bits of vegetation cemented together with a special
kidney secretion. After the nest is constructed, the male performs a
courtship dance, which stimulates a female to respond. Her re-
sponse triggers further courtship by the male until he escorts her to
the nest. She deposits her eggs there and then leaves. The male
fertilizes the eggs and remains to guard the nest, and later the young.
The details of the nest construction vary with the species but the
general patterns are similar.

Brook sticklebacks often inhabit cold, leech-infested waters, but to
the intrepid fish watcher they offer great possibilities. Frequently
you can find the nests by looking for males defending them. Wade
along slowly until you see a dark fish that stands its ground as you
approach. If he is defending a territory, you will see that he chases

all other fish away from an area a yard or so across. The nest will be somewhere in that area. It will look like a little knot of vegetation an inch to an inch and a half in diameter. Usually it will be attached to bullrushes or elodea a few inches off the bottom. The male will stand by the nest even when you approach it closely. Back off and watch the process. From time to time the male will enter the nest to fan the eggs inside. To watch sticklebacks on a warm sunny day in June is to witness natural history at its best.

Temperate Basses
(Family Moronidae)

Temperate basses are silvery spiny-rayed fishes with rough scales, two dorsal fins that may be slightly joined, and pectoral fins with nearly vertical bases. They have three spines at the front of the anal fin. There are four species in North America, two in Europe.

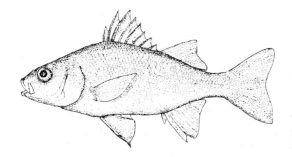

The white perch, *Morone americana*, is abundant in coastal estuaries and now in Lake Ontario.

A funny thing about common names—some are very precise and descriptive, others quite misleading. The striped bass, white bass, and yellow bass belong to the family Moronidae, which also includes the white perch (not to be confused with the yellow perch, a member of the family Percidae). The largemouth and smallmouth basses, though, belong to the sunfish family, Centrarchidae.

The striped bass, *Morone saxatilis*, is one of the most important game fishes of North America. It is native to the Atlantic and Gulf coasts, and it has been successfully introduced to the Pacific Coast as well. Landlocked strains have been introduced into inland lakes across the continent.

Usually the striped bass is an anadromous fish, moving into fresh waters to spawn near the boundary between fresh and salt water, where the eggs are kept in suspension by the dense brackish water. After spending their first summer or two in the rivers, the young move into the ocean, where they grow rapidly. In their third or fourth year, when they have reached maturity, they return to the river to spawn. Long-lived fishes, they have been known to reach weights of more than 100 pounds.

The white perch, *Morone americana,* is small but abundant in some brackish waters. It can live in full salt water or in purely fresh water. Recently it became established in Lake Ontario, where it has become very abundant. It is found in Lake Erie and Lake Michigan as well.

The white bass, *Morone chrysops,* is strictly a freshwater species. It travels in schools and often feeds at the surface on emerging insects. A large school creates a spectacular disturbance as the fishes' momentum carries them past their targets. Fishing for white bass then becomes a matter of hunting for schools in their feeding frenzies.

Perches
(Family Percidae)

Perches are typical spiny-rayed fishes with two dorsal fins, rough scales, and one spine and five rays in the thoracic pelvic fins. Unlike the river basses, they have one or two spines, not three, in the anal fins. The lateral line is variable, incomplete in some species, and it does not extend onto the base of the caudal fin. This large family includes the yellow perch, the walleye, the sauger, and some 150 small, colorful species called darters. These fishes live in fresh water in Europe as well as in North America. Recently a small European species called the ruffe has become established in lakes Superior and Michigan. It could become a pest in the next few years. From the standpoint of the inland angler, perches certainly rank among our most important fishes.

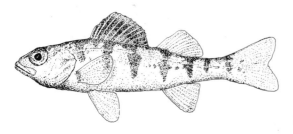

The yellow perch, *Perca flavescens.*

The Large Perches

Among the larger species, the walleye, *Stizostedion vitreum,* is a sport fisher's dream. It can weigh as much as 25 pounds and is a good fighter that responds to artificial and natural baits. Walleyes are the mainstay of many of the nation's lakes and larger reservoirs. Recently the zander, the European cognate of the walleye, has been introduced in a few places.

The blue pike of Lake Erie and perhaps Lake Ontario, once a popular sport and commercial species, is now extinct. It is usually considered to have been a subspecies of the walleye, from which it differed in eye size as well as color. Apparently it was unable to compete with the walleye when the environment of the lake began to change as a result of human impact. Perhaps the walleye was more adaptable, although it, too, had its troubles—it was quite scarce in Lake Erie in the early 1960s. The walleye has come back, but the blue pike never did. Even earlier, the related sauger, *Stizostedion canadense,* also became commercially extinct in Lake Erie. The reasons for the sauger's decline are not clear, but it appears that overfishing was involved, along with the destruction of spawning areas by silt deposits that resulted from erosion of the land as the forests were cleared for agriculture.

When you say "fish" to many people, the yellow perch is the fish they think of. The perch is illustrated in so many biology textbooks and dissected in so many school laboratories that we have come to think of it as the "typical" fish. In many areas old *Perca flavescens* is *the* fish. Easy to catch, plentiful, good to eat, and attractive to look at, it has it all. Perch are interesting to the fish watcher, too. In the clear waters of northern lakes they are easy to see around rocks and seawalls near shore. Yellow perch spawn in the early spring, laying their eggs in zigzag rows embedded in gelatinous ribbons draped over underwater structures. Sometimes segments of these ribbons wash up on shore, exciting the curiosity of beachcombers.

Darters

The males of many of the roughly 150 species of darters develop almost unbelievable colors during their breeding seasons. Darters have a variety of spawning habits; some lay their eggs in gravel, some spawn on plants, and others carefully deposit their eggs on vertical surfaces or even on the undersides of rocks. Since many species live in small creeks and spawn in shallow water, their court-ship can be readily observed by the fish watcher who doesn't mind getting out early in the spring with a view box. Most darters live in rather swift streams, but some, such as the johnny and tessellated darters and the Iowa darter, live in lakes and ponds as well.

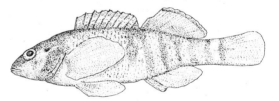

The rainbow darter, *Etheostoma cae-ruleum.*

Darters are fun to watch even when they are not breeding. They have small swim bladders and spend most of their time resting on the bottom. I can remember lying on the bank of a creek as a boy trying to decide whether the organisms I now know to have been johnny darters were fish or some kind of amphibian.

The logperch, *Percina caprodes,* one of the larger darters, inhabits lakes as well as streams. It uses the distinctive conical snout over-hanging its mouth to flip over pebbles and uncover tasty organisms.

In the northern states the logperch spawns as late as July. The males congregate on shallow sandbars. When a female is ready to spawn, she moves into the shallows and is immediately surrounded by several males. After the brief frenzy of the spawning act, the female returns to deep water and the males resume feeding, probably consuming some of the eggs in the process.

Most darters live in rather swift and clear creeks. Some, however, live in slow waters. One such fish is the Iowa darter, *Etheostoma exile*, which lives in clear cool lakes in the northern states and Canada; another is the Arkansas darter, *Etheostoma cragini*, which lives in spring-fed creeks of the high plains.

Kansas, 1952

The source of the stream in which we wash our fossils is an artesian spring at the north end of the park. This particular spring consists of a number of "boils" where the water reaches the surface. The boils show as spots of clear sand six inches to a foot or so in diameter, kept clean by the upwelling water, which also separates the sand grains so that they can support no weight. A stick thrust into one of the boils would sink of its own weight. We have heard stories of stray cows and even herds of buffalo getting caught in the spring and disappearing forever. As it turns out, this spring is the habitat of the Arkansas darter, Etheostoma cragini, *and I have spent many evenings after work watching the darters by the beam of a flashlight. The spring is also the home of abundant planarian flatworms, some of which I collect and preserve for a colleague back at the University of Michigan.* Etheostoma cragini *is small and overall bicolored, brownish above and white to orange below with black flecks. It is not an especially pretty darter, but it certainly lives in interesting places.*

Sunfishes
(Family Centrarchidae)

The centrarchids include the sunfishes and the black basses, including the largemouth and the smallmouth. They are spiny rayed fishes with the dorsal fins joined by membranes, although the fin is deeply notched in the largemouth bass. They are colorful fishes of slower waters. All sunfishes have at least a trace of a spot on the

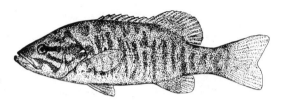

The smallmouth bass, *Micropterus dolomieu.*

upper operculum, or gill coverings, and all but one are nest builders. They have thoracic pelvic fins and vertical pectoral fin bases, and all except the mud sunfish have rough scales. They have three to eleven anal fin spines.

If fish watchers were to design a family of fishes specifically for their own use, this would be the result. Centrarchids are uniquely North American, although they have been introduced into other parts of the world—not always to the benefit of the native species. Only one species of centrarchid is native to the region west of the Rocky Mountains. This is the Sacramento perch, *Archoplites interruptus,* and interestingly enough, it does not build a nest like those of the rest of the family.

Sunfishes, including the largemouth and smallmouth basses (the so-called black basses), the crappies, and rock bass, and the flyer, are rather advanced perciform fishes with spiny fin rays, rough scales, and vertical pectoral fin bases. The basses are elongate, although their bodies are robust and suggest power and speed, whereas the sunfishes have deep compressed bodies that are adapted for maneuverability. The sunfish shape is vividly expressed in the name of one of the most widespread fishes, the pumpkinseed. Perhaps the sunfishes owe their common name to their colorfulness and to their shallow-water habitats.

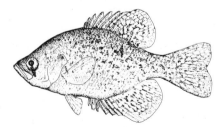

The black crappie, *Pomoxis nigromaculatus.*

Sunfishes are easy to catch, good fighters, and fine eating. Their primary benefit to the fish watcher is the fact that they build nests and carry out their courtship and breeding in broad daylight in shallow water near shore, even in urban areas where foot traffic is heavy along the shore.

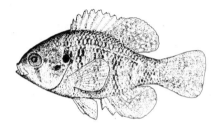

The banded sunfish, *Enneacanthus obesus.*

Sunfish nests are built by the males. The nest is a shallow depression a foot or more in diameter, created by vigorous fanning of the bottom. While the male is building the nest, the females promenade back and forth in the general area. When the male is satisfied with the nest, he begins to posture near it, and if he is in luck, a female responds. Ultimately she accompanies him to the nest and they roll against each other as they release the eggs and sperm. The fertilized eggs drop into crevices between the pebbles on the bottom. After spawning the female departs, leaving the male to guard the nest and its developing eggs against all intruders. Often a male will resume his courtship, so that a single nest can contain eggs in various stages of development. Recently Dr. Wallace Dominey found that small males that are unable to defend their own territories are able to participate in the spawning by assuming the coloration of a female and joining the spawning pair. It appeared to onlookers—and doubtless to the first male, too—as though he were spawning with two females. This ruse has now been seen among other species of sunfishes.

Each species of sunfish can be expected to have a slightly different spawning procedure. Notice that species differ in the time and location of spawning, the depth of the water, the type of bottom, the position of males on the nest, and the degree to which they tolerate close neighbors. Bluegills are colonial nesters, and sometimes their nests are so close together that the individual depressions are hexagonal rather than round. Other species may not allow other nests within a yard or more.

Don't miss the sunfish spawning!

Pygmy Sunfishes
(Family Elassomatidae)

Pygmy sunfishes are often put in the family Centrarchidae. They are tiny, swamp-dwelling fishes of the American South and Southeast, with no lateral line and no sensory canals on the lower jaw. The scales are smooth and they have a reduced number of dorsal fin spines and caudal rays. Several of the internal skull bones are also absent. These dwarf sunfishes superficially resemble some of the tropical killifishes, but structurally they are diminutive basses. Perhaps their unique features are associated with their small size.

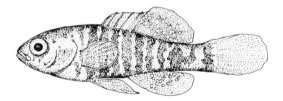

The banded pygmy sunfish, *Elassoma zonatum*.

Cichlids
(Family Cichlidae)

Cichlids, from the southern hemisphere, are popular aquarium fishes, and several species have been introduced into the United States. One species is native, however, although its natural range barely reaches southern Texas. Many cichlids resemble our sunfishes, but their lateral line is discontinuous at about the level of the beginning of the second dorsal fin.

The Rio Grande cichlid, *Cichlasoma cyanoguttatum,* is the only native species of the family Cichlidae in the United States. Its natural

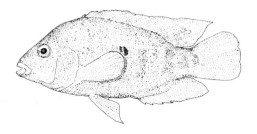

The Rio Grande cichlid, *Cichlasoma cyanoguttatum.*

range was the Rio Grande drainage of Texas and northeastern Mexico. It has been successfully introduced into other parts of Texas and also into central Florida.

This is a very pretty fish, generally dark greenish gray, with brilliant blue-green spots. A dark smudge under the second dorsal fin of the young is sometimes called the mark of St. Peter's thumb. Sometimes it appears as the first of four to six vertically elongate blotches on the rear half of the side. The lateral line is discontinuous under the last half of the dorsal fin.

Sometimes called Rio Grande perch (although it is not a percid), this species lives in vegetated areas of creeks and small rivers.

Drums
(Family Sciaenidae)

Most drums are coastal marine fishes but one species is widespread in North American fresh waters. Sometimes called the sheepshead, the freshwater drum, *Aplodinotus grunniens,* is a rather typical drum with a blunt, overhanging snout, a long second dorsal fin, large sensory canals on the head, and rough scales. The lateral line continues out to the tips of the longest rays of the asymmetrically pointed tail. It tends to be silvery gray to brownish, sometimes with a light orange tint on the pelvic fins. The first ray of the pelvic fins is extended as a short filament.

The sheepshead is a fish of large lakes and rivers, but because it comes into shallow water, it can sometimes be seen from shore. It is not a choice food fish and people who catch them sometimes discard

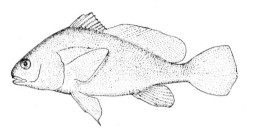

An immature male freshwater drum, *Aplodinotus grunniens*, 15½ inches long. Redrawn from *A Biological Survey of the Lake Ontario Watershed* (Albany: State of New York Conservation Department, 1940), plate 4.

them, so that their carcasses frequently are found on shore. They are well worth examining. The bone that covers the head canals is reduced to narrow bridges, giving the skull a delicately sculptured appearance. Drums have molar-like pharyngeal teeth attached to thick triangular pharyngeal bones. Each tooth of a large drum can be nearly a quarter of an inch in diameter. The otoliths, or ear bones, lie deep inside the skull and are very large. If you shake a well-cleaned and dry skull you can hear them rattle. The otoliths enable the fish to detect the pull of gravity, and thus to maintain its upright position. To remove the otoliths you may have to break open the neurocranium, or braincase. In a fish a foot or so long, each otolith is about the diameter of a dime but much thicker. The otoliths are made of translucent whitish calcium carbonate. A deep groove on one face of the otolith looks like a carved letter *L* (backward on the other otolith). Some people carry large drum otoliths as "lucky stones."

The drum is one of the few freshwater species that lays its eggs in open water. There the tiny transparent eggs drift with the currents. This is one reason that drums are confined to lakes and slow-moving rivers.

In some areas drums are quite abundant, and state fish and game organizations have tried to encourage people to fish for them, but they are not particularly good to eat.

Sculpins
(Family Cottidae)

The family Cottidae is a large family with numerous species in fresh waters and even more in the sea. They are related to the

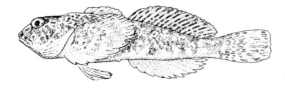

The slimy sculpin, *Cottus cognatus.*

marine scorpionfishes and searobins, with which they share a bony strut that connects the bones around the eye with the cheekbone. In sculpins this "bony stay" is embedded in the skin and not easily seen. Sculpins have few or no scales, although some species have bony prickles in the skin. The first dorsal fin has slender and flexible spines and the bases of the pectoral fins slope backward. The pelvic fins are far forward with a minute, embedded spine and three of four rays. Sculpins have large terminal mouths and moderately large eyes.

Freshwater sculpins are rather small fishes with huge pectoral fins. Most of our species live in streams, but two or three live in deep waters of the Great Lakes and other northern lakes. Some scientists have been using the Johnson Sea-Link submersible vehicle to study the habits of the deep-water sculpin of Lake Superior, but stream sculpins are the only ones that fish watchers are likely to see.

Sculpins tend to be quite secretive, but often you can find them by turning over rocks in shallow streams. Males guard nests under rocks. The yellow-orange eggs are quite large. With a view box to get rid of surface ripples, you can walk right up to the nests.

Soles
(Family Soleidae)

The flatfishes, which include the flounders, soles, and halibuts, are mostly saltwater fishes, but one species, the hogchoker, *Trinectes maculatus*, enters estuaries and sometimes lives in fresh water. Soles are small, rounded flatfishes with small eyes on the right side of the head.

The hogchoker is a small species, rarely reaching 6 inches in

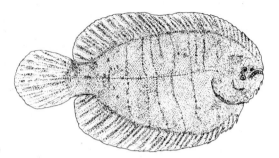

The hogchoker, *Trinectes maculatus.*

length. Like other flatfishes, it is a master at camouflage, able to match its background to a remarkable degree. Small hogchokers are a delight in the aquarium. They have a tendency to cling to the sides of the tank and even to the surface of the water as if it were the bottom. Try snorkeling in an estuary on a hot summer day. You probably won't see hogchokers unless they move.

5   *The Biology of Fishes*

Fishes face the same problems that all other organisms face. The main objectives of each individual are to complete its life cycle and to produce offspring that continue the next round of the life cycle.

In theory this individual faces only a few simple problems. First, it must find and remain in a proper physical and chemical environment—one with the right temperature, enough oxygen, and enough water with an acceptable chemical composition to live in and to carry away waste products such as carbon dioxide, nitrogenous wastes, and fecal materials. Its environment must also be free of toxic substances, natural or synthetic. Second, the organism must be able to find and capture appropriate food in adequate quantities for maintenance, growth, and reproduction. Third, it must be able to avoid predators, including disease organisms. Fourth, it must be able to find mates and suitable conditions for reproduction. All of these programs have to be carried out more or less simultaneously in a climate of competition for the available resources. How organisms share resources is the subject of all of ecology, including fish watching.

More Fish Anatomy

The fish body plan is not too different from our own except that fish have gills instead of lungs. The fish takes in water through the mouth by moving its cheeks outward to reduce pressure in the

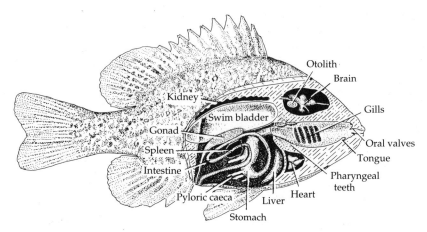

Internal anatomy of the pumpkinseed.

mouth, so that water is drawn in. Then the cheeks move inward and the gill covers move outward, forcing water past the gills, which extract oxygen, and pulling it into the gill chamber. Finally the gill covers move inward, forcing the water out through the gill opening. The gill membranes and the oral valves, small bands of membrane just behind the teeth, serve to ensure that the water flows in the proper direction.

Fishes also have a swim bladder, which is a gas-filled chamber. As the fish descends through the water, the water pressure compresses the gas and the fish loses buoyancy. When gas is added to the swim bladder, its volume increases and the fish becomes more buoyant. In this way the fish can maintain neutral buoyancy at any depth. Gas (mainly oxygen) is secreted from the bloodstream by a special gas gland. Some lower fishes have a duct connecting the gut with the swim bladder, and they can gulp air at the surface to fill the swim bladder or expel gas as they ascend so that the swim bladder does not overexpand. The swim bladder of gars and bowfins serves as a lung, which probably was its original function in evolutionary history. In some bottom-living darters the swim bladder is reduced or lost entirely.

The fish's heart is simpler than a mammal's—it has only two chambers rather than four. Blood enters the atrium, passes into the muscular ventricle, and is pumped out almost directly into the gills. From the gills it flows to the dorsal aortae and is carried to all parts of the body. The capillaries in the gills reduce the pressure, so that in general fish have rather low blood pressure.

How Smart Are Fish?

No one has suggested that fish are profound philosophers, but as vertebrate animals they have nervous systems similar to ours and they certainly are capable of responding to environmental cues and of learning what they need to know. The goldfish in your aquarium learn when and where to expect to be fed.

A fish's eyes are adapted for seeing in water. They focus by moving the lens rather than by changing its shape, as ours do, but in general the basic structure is quite similar to ours. Fish can see color to some extent. Touch and temperature receptors are located in the skin. Fish detect odors by pumping water through the nostrils and over a special sensory tissue. Taste buds are not confined to the tongue, as ours are, but are scattered over much of the outside surface of the body and sometimes are concentrated in special structures such as the barbels of catfishes. Fish lack the middle and exterior ear, but in some the swim bladder and sometimes the anterior vertebrae are modified to conduct sound directly to the inner ear. They have semicircular canals like ours that detect motion in three dimensions. Enlarged sacs in the semicircular canal system contain otoliths, calcareous structures that rest on sensory hairlike structures. As the fish tilts, the otolith rests on different areas, and these differences tell the fish how it is oriented with respect to gravity.

Fishes also have special sensory systems that we do not. One is the lateral line system, which is a porous tube running along the side of the body. Hairlike structures in the tube respond to vibrations in the water which are transmitted to the fluid in the tube through the pores. This special system enables the fish to detect sound in the water.

Some fishes have electroreceptor organs that permit them to detect very weak electrical currents, and a few groups of fishes in other parts of the world even have organs that produce electrical fields, which they use for navigation and for detection of prey.

Fish are able to detect pressure in a way that we humans, living as we do in a two-dimensional world, cannot do effectively. They can sense low levels of oxygen in the water and respond by increasing their gill movements.

So how smart are fish? If we gauge smartness by the ability to reason and think things through and write poetry, then we cannot call them very smart. But if we gauge it by the ability to monitor and respond to one's environment, maintain one's internal physiology, and learn simple tasks, then fish do pretty well.

Life Histories

Every parent knows that the difference between an adult and a child is much more than a matter of age. Children are disciples of a different philosopher and their view of reality has little concordance with adult doctrines. So it is with fish. The life history consists of several distinct stages. In the first stage, the embryo in the fertilized egg is essentially self-contained. When the individual hatches from the egg it enters a larval stage that may be precisely adapted for a

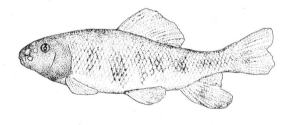

The creek chubsucker, *Erimyzon oblongus*.

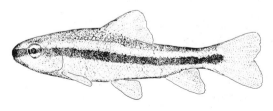

The juvenile chubsucker, *Erimyzon oblongus*.

particular set of conditions. The end of the larval period is marked by a sharp transition to the juvenile stage. The juvenile differs from the adult in its size, its color, and its interest in sex: it hasn't any. At last comes the mature, reproducing adult stage, which usually lasts as long as the fish lives. Some species have a definite prejuvenile stage between the larva and the juvenile.

If life has a purpose, it is to keep the cycle going. The variations on this simple theme are seemingly endless. The survival of the species depends on continuation of the cycle, and it can continue only if individuals survive long enough to mature and reproduce at least once.

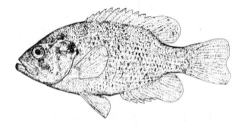

The rock bass, *Ambloplites rupestris.*

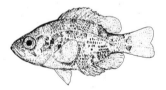

The juvenile rock bass, *Ambloplites rupestris.*

Each stage in the life cycle has its own set of environmental requirements for food, shelter, and companionship, so must fishes change their habitat as they mature. An environment that is perfect for larvae may not do at all for juveniles, and juveniles are not necessarily equipped to survive in the adult world. A few examples:

- Young American shad live in fresh water. As they mature they gradually work their way downstream until they reach the ocean at the end of their first summer.
- Baby trout have bold bands of color on their sides. These so-called parr marks disappear as they get bigger.

- Newly hatched bowfins have suckers on the tips of their snouts. (They stick around the nests.)
- Baby bullheads crowd into dense schools, herded together by their parents.
- Newly hatched suckers have upturned mouths and travel near the surface of the water. Their mouths change as they grow, and they sink to become bottom dwellers.
- Juvenile chubsuckers have bold longitudinal stripes that break into short vertical bars as they get bigger.
- Young rock bass have squarish blotches that make them look like little checkerboards, but adults have rows of spots.
- Breeding adults often develop transient secondary sex characters. The males of many of our minnows and darters become highly colorful during the breeding season.

Spawning migrations ensure that the eggs are laid in environments that are favorable for the early life stages. These migrations range from the famous salmon runs that involve trips of hundreds or thousands of miles down to movements of a few feet as the spawners move from pools to riffles in streams. In each case the result is the same: the eggs are deposited where the young will have the best chance to survive.

A visit to a trout hatchery provides a good chance to see the differences in the life stages. In late fall or early winter you may be lucky enough to see the staff taking eggs and setting them up in troughs in the hatchery building.

Fishes have a lot of ways of going about their courtship and breeding. They differ not only in their migration patterns but in their courtship rituals, in their nest-building habits, in the time they spawn, and in the types of eggs they lay. Some produce large and colorful eggs; others lay eggs that are tiny and transparent. The eggs and larvae of most marine fishes drift freely in mid-water, but most freshwater fishes lay eggs that sink to the bottom. Often the eggs have a sticky surface so that they adhere to the bottom wherever they fall. Some adults place their eggs carefully on surfaces that they have cleaned.

Reproductive specializations help organisms avoid interference from other species. If they all spawned in the same area at the same time, some would be driven from the nesting sites or otherwise prevented from spawning. Specializations that permit each species to meet its basic needs in its own way are considered mechanisms for sharing the available resources. These mechanisms make it possible for many species to live together. In other words, they are partial explanations for the diversity of species in the natural world.

A Class Project

For several summers I served as a visiting professor at the University of Michigan Biological Station, in the northern part of Michigan's Lower Peninsula, teaching a course in fish biology to graduate and advanced undergraduate students. University field stations give students the opportunity to study organisms, from parasites to microalgae to birds and mammals, at firsthand. One of the students' favorite projects was to culture the eggs of the trout-perch, a small fish that spawned on the sandy shoals right in front of the laboratory. Other species could have been used, but the trout-perch were abundant and were spawning at the time the summer session was in full swing. The adults were caught in a small net as they came in after dark. If they were fully ripe, gentle pressure on the female's abdomen would result in a free flow of transparent eggs. We rinsed a clean Petri dish with water from the lake where the adults were taken, then stripped a few dozen eggs into the moist dish. We added some of the whitish milt from a male and gently mixed the eggs and sperms thoroughly. We then added a half-inch or so of lake water, returned the adults to their habitat, placed the dish on the stage of a low-power dissecting microscope, and sat back to watch the process. In a few minutes the fertilized eggs water-hardened—that is, the outer membrane became swollen and separated from the rest of the egg. In an hour or so the eggs started to divide. Unlike the frog eggs that we studied in high school biology, most fish eggs have the cell material confined to a small button on the side of the yolk. Since the yolk itself does not divide, the only evidence of cell division was the formation of a furrow across the germinal disk area. As development proceeded the cells became too small to see even with the microscope and the germinal disk took on a frothy appearance. At that point we checked on the eggs every few hours, replacing about half the water each time we checked them. Any eggs that had become opaque were dead and we removed them, because dead eggs are soon attacked by a fungus that will spread to the healthy eggs. It is also important to keep the temperature of the developing eggs as close as possible to the temperature of the water where they were spawned, and to avoid exposing them to long periods of bright light.

Over the next few days we witnessed dramatic changes as the eggs developed. After a few hours the embryo appeared as a double ridge across the germinal disk. Later the head began to form as a swelling at one end of the ridge. Soon the eyes became visible as transparent bubbles (the retinal pigments did not develop until later). Behind the eyes were some tiny bubbles that marked the developing ears. The body divided into segments and the tail bud separated from the yolk surface. One of the most exciting parts of the process came when the heart appeared and started to beat. When we peered through the microscope and saw the red corpuscles streaming through the pumping heart, we knew that the embryo really was alive. About this time the embryo started to move, alternately wriggling violently and resting almost motionless. Some pigment cells began to form, and in a few days the tiny embryos hatched in a burst of energy as they struggled to free themselves from the egg membranes. Not all of them made it; some simply did not have the strength to escape the membrane that until then had protected them.

After hatching, young fish survive for a time on the remaining yolk, but eventually they have to start feeding on their own. This is another critical period when many hatchlings die. The best chance of our specimens' survival was in the lake where they came from, and reluctantly we released them.

A word of caution: If you try to hatch some fish eggs and if your baby fish do survive and you want to release them, be sure to put them back where the parents came from, not in the nearest convenient ditch. This way they will have the best chance for survival and you won't be responsible for introducing them into a place where they might later become pests.

Reproductive Diversity

Natural reproduction is the only way to produce more fish. It is a very complex process and conditions have to be just right, for there is little margin for error. The fish have to find their way to the spawning grounds and locate and court mates, and the eggs have to be fertilized and deposited in a favorable environment. The complex development of the embryo and its hatching have to proceed according to plan, and then the hatchlings have to find the right kind of food and shelter. Everything has to happen at the right time, and the weather has to cooperate.

Most fishes in temperate climates have rather short spawning seasons of a week or two. If everything goes exactly right, they produce large numbers of young, and that age group (in fishes it is called a year class) is represented by many individuals. If any part of the process goes wrong, that year class will be scarce or absent.

Most of the smaller fishes have relatively short life spans. They live only two or three years and thus spawn only once or twice. Two or three bad years in a row can result in real trouble for the species, but with a good year the species can recover very quickly. Long-lived fishes, such as the lake sturgeon, may not spawn until they are more than ten years old. Their recovery from a disaster that reduces their numbers can take a very long time.

It is not unusual for two or more species to use the same spawning grounds at the same time. I know a stream in northern Michigan where one can stand on the bank and watch white suckers spawning over the same gravel bars where sea lampreys have built their nests. Nearby is a small lake where the shallows are dotted with groups of logperch spawning during the day and trout-perch spawning at night. In streams the stone-pile nests of creek chubs and river chubs are often used by other minnow species, including common shiners and rosyface shiners. Occasionally, when several species spawn in the same area at the same time, mistakes occur and some eggs get fertilized by sperm from a different species. Usually such eggs fail to develop at all, but sometimes development starts and then ceases later in the process. Occasionally development goes to completion and the resulting hybrids survive. A few even reproduce, but most are sterile.

Let's think about this a little. If suitable spawning sites are in short supply, then such accidents become more frequent. Furthermore, if the nest builders are too crowded, they destroy one another's nests. With fewer offspring hatching and surviving, there will be fewer reproducing adults when their turn comes, and more of the nests will be successful. This is one important kind of population control, and it has great significance in maintaining population levels and the balance of the species that live together.

Most species have rather specific requirements, and once you have seen fish of a certain species spawn, you will be able to predict where and when those fish will spawn the next year. Try to detect subtle differences in the environments in which various species spawn—differences in depth, current, shade, bottom type, and so on—that act to keep the species separated. The sunfishes are a good group to practice on. Most ponds have more than one species, and though their nesting habits are generally similar, they are not identical. See if you can discover how they differ.

Many small fishes nest in holes or crevices under logs or rocks. Frequently you will be able to locate a nest by watching the behavior of the parent guarding it. We have found fathead minnows and madtom catfishes guarding discarded beer cans that they had appropriated for their nests. Whenever you see a highly colored fish chasing other fish of the same or different species from a well-defined area, take a good look to see if you can locate its nest. Once you find one, you will know where to look for others.

Fish eggs are very nutritious (after all, the yolk is stored food for the embryo) and much sought after by other fishes, not necessarily of different species. Much of the effort put forth by guarding parents is directed at chasing fishes that are trying to eat the eggs. In the late spring and early summer, when schools of logperch, *Percina caprodes,* spawn on sandy shallow areas; schools of males (they can be recognized by the dark pigment on their heads and dorsal fins) cruise along the edge of the drop-off while females remain in deeper water. When a female is ready to spawn, she moves into the shallows. There a group of males spawn with her in a frenzy that pushes her into the sand as the eggs and sperms are released. Most of the eggs are buried and quickly become covered with sand grains that stick to the outside of the egg, but any eggs that are not buried quickly are eaten by the males or by sand shiners that follow the spawning groups in the hope of an easy meal.

Later in the season, when the newly hatched young emerge from their nests, many spend the first few weeks of their free lives in rather tight schools near the surface. Young white suckers are especially conspicuous when they are half to three-fourths of an inch long. Then their habits change and they sink to the bottom and disperse.

Freshwater fishes have a wide spectrum of spawning habits. Here are a few that you can see with a little patience:

- Broadcast eggs over vegetation with no parental care: pike, pickerel, carp, goldfish.
- Spawn over sand with no parental care: logperch (day), trout-perch (night).
- Spawn in streams over gravel with no parental care: sucker.
- Spawn in rock crevices with no parental care: satinfin and spotfin shiners.
- Spawn under rocks with male guarding eggs: sculpin, fantail darter, bluntnose minnow.
- Males fan out shallow saucer-shaped depressions: sunfish, black bass.
- Males build pebble mounds: river chub, hornyhead chub, creek chub, fallfish, cutlips minnow.
- Males build nests of vegetation: stickleback.
- Eggs pelagic (floating free in the water): freshwater drum.
- Eggs in gelatinous zigzag ribbons: yellow perch.
- Eggs bright yellow and laid in pancake-shaped masses in crevices or other shelter: bullhead catfish.
- Eggs black: sturgeon.
- Both parents guard eggs and young: catfish, bullhead.

Age and Growth

Unlike mammals, which stop growing at maturity, fish continue to grow throughout their lives, although the growth slows to almost nothing after a certain size is reached. Growth rates are greatly influenced by environmental conditions. Goldfish kept in small containers remain small even though they are given abundant food. If these goldfish are later released into a pond, they will start to grow again until they begin to approach the maximum size for the species. Fishbones grow by the accretion of concentric layers, a process that leaves a record of the individual's growth history in each bone. Scales and otoliths (calcareous structures in the fish's ear) usually are the easiest to read, and scales can be removed for study with little harm to the fish. Such investigations are very powerful tools for the fish manager because a study of the growth history can determine growth rates and provide a great deal of information about the life history which can be related to environmental conditions.

The aging of fishes that have lived in temperate waters where seasons are clearly defined is relatively easy to trace. Scales grow by adding rings, called circuli, to the outer margin. As water temperatures begin to drop in the late summer and fall, the rings get closer together and finally cease to be formed when winter sets in. In the spring, when temperatures start to rise and food becomes abundant, more rings are added. As the fish is growing rapidly now, these rings tend to be spaced quite far apart. Often the last ring to be formed in the fall is incomplete and the first spring circulus appears to cut across it. One problem for the biologist reading the scales is that other events—severe storms, injuries, abnormally high water temperatures, spawning—may also interrupt normal growth and produce a change in the patterns of the rings called a false annulus. Sometimes spawning checks are more pronounced than the true annuli. Scale readers learn to recognize the differences.

A fish's scales record its entire growth history. Once the scales form on the young fish, no more scales are added (but scales that are lost will be replaced). Thus the relationship between the length of the scale and the length of the fish remains constant. By measuring a projected image of the scale, researchers can calculate how long the fish was at the end of each year of its life. This is a powerful research tool. By tracing the growth history of numbers of fish we can determine which years produced good growth and which were bad years, at what age fish grow fastest, and so on. When we want to know the age of a fish that has no scales, such as a catfish, we can examine cross sections of the pectoral fin spines or vertebrae.

A few years ago it was discovered that rings are added to the otoliths, those calcareous deposits in the ear, every day. Now we can even determine the number of days a very young fish has lived.

Food and Feeding

Some fish are picky eaters; others are constitutionally gluttonous. Most fishes are lazy and will take whatever is easiest to catch and still acceptable as food. Anglers take advantage of this fact when they choose baits and lures.

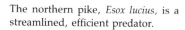
The northern pike, *Esox lucius,* is a streamlined, efficient predator.

Few fish are strict vegetarians. They probably couldn't be if they wanted to, because most plants have animals associated with them and fishes lack enzymes to digest cellulose effectively. Fish that feed primarily on plant material have some sort of mechanism, either specialized teeth or a gizzard-like stomach, to grind the plants and crush the cell walls.

Fish are anatomically specialized to concentrate on some particular way of feeding. Bottom feeders, such as suckers and sturgeons, have their mouths located on the undersides of their heads. Surface feeders, such as killifishes and silversides, have mouths that are turned upward. More generalized carnivores have mouths that are more or less at the midline of the body.

The longnose gar has long jaws and needlelike teeth suited for capturing fish prey.

The shape of a fish's body also contributes to its feeding style. Sculpins lie still on the bottom and under rocks, waiting for their prey to come close enough to be inhaled with a mouthful of water. Pikes and pickerels wait for the prey to get within striking distance. Sunfishes, with their short deep bodies, are able to turn quickly and outmaneuver their insect prey. The coloration of the fishes not only allows them to sneak up on or ambush their prey but also protects them from their predators.

Fishes have three series of teeth. The most visible are the outer teeth of the upper and lower jaws. The second series consists of teeth on the tongue and the roof of the mouth. The third series is made up of the upper pharyngeal teeth, between the upper ends of the gill arch, and the lower pharyngeal teeth, in the floor of the pharynx, just behind the gills.

Piscivorous fishes, such as the gars and the pikes, have sharp, pointed teeth in the jaws and the roof of the mouth. Fishes that feed on insects and other invertebrates have bands of short, bluntly pointed teeth that both grasp their prey and crush it. The freshwater drum has heavy, molar-like pharyngeal teeth that can be used to crush mollusk shells.

Minnows and suckers have no teeth at all in their mouths; they process their food with their highly specialized lower pharyngeal teeth. (See the illustration on p. 112).

The gill arches are also part of the feeding mechanism. Rows of bony projections called rakers (they resemble the teeth of a garden rake) along the fronts of the gill arches strain the water that is taken in the mouth and passed over the gills. The gill rakers are short and widely spaced in carnivores, but numerous, long, and close-set in plankton feeders, who use them as a sieve for gathering their tiny prey.

Studies of the food habits of fishes show that even the most specialized feeders frequently feed on prey that doesn't appear to match the fishes' obvious specializations. The reason is that fishes tend to conserve their energy, and feed on whatever is easiest to catch. When times are hard and food is scarce, however, the specializations become effective, and the prey matches the feeding adaptations. By feeding on items that other species can't use, the specialist gains a competitive advantage.

Defense

Because fish are considered good to eat by birds, snakes, turtles, alligators, mammals, and other fishes, they are always in danger of being eaten by something. As a result, nearly everything they do is somehow governed, or at least limited, by the need to be wary of predators. This problem works against the fish watcher, because the fish have no way of distinguishing between a friendly fish watcher and someone bent on making a meal of them. The surest way of avoiding predation is to avoid the feeding grounds of potential predators altogether. That is why we never see some species. They simply have enough sense to stay away from the dangerous shallow waters. The second line of defense is to flee, so we see fish heading for deeper and safer waters as we try to approach them in the shallows. The third tactic is to freeze and remain motionless in the hope that the predator will fail to recognize them as prey. This tactic actually favors the fish watcher because it is exactly what we want the fish to do—hold still so we can get a good look at it.

From the fish's standpoint, of course, it is best to avoid being caught by a predator in the first place, but evasion is certainly not possible all the time, so fishes have evolved a variety of structural and behavioral ways to frustrate their predators. Among them at thick and hard scales (gars, bowfins), strong spines (sticklebacks, sunfishes), poisonous spines (madtoms), large size (sturgeons), and distasteful or poisonous slime or flesh (extremely rare among our freshwater fishes).

Structural adaptations for defense have to be correlated with behavior. It would do a fish no good to freeze, for example, if it did not also have a cryptic color pattern or at least a combination of color and shape that would fool the predator into eliminating it from further consideration as a meal candidate.

Since the prey must defend itself and the predator must eat, and since all predators are prey to other predators, conflicts are inevitable. What happens when a fish sees a desirable prey that is in range of another species that is a potential predator? If the fish is too conservative, it will starve to death; if it is too reckless, it will be eaten. Much fish watching consists of witnessing the solutions to just such conflicts.

Counting Fish

Sometimes when you find a place where you can see a whole school of fish, you begin to wonder how many fish are in the school. From there it is a short jump to wondering how many fish are in the lake or the stream. This question is at the heart of fish management and conservation. How can we count the fish in a particular body of water? Since direct counts are seldom possible, biologists have to settle for indirect methods. Sometimes they are able to count the fish that come to the spawning grounds. Sometimes they can count the fish in part of the body of water, and if they have reason to believe that the fish are evenly distributed, they can extrapolate from the partial volume to the whole volume. Usually fish managers are less interested in an exact count than in knowing whether the population is increasing or decreasing, and for this purpose they use catch per unit effort, or CPUE: they keep a record of the number of fish caught and the effort required to catch them, such as the number of hours a particular type of trap is set, the number of hours of fishing done by anglers, or the number of net hauls made by commercial fishers. Then CPUEs taken months apart can be compared to indicate whether the fish are becoming more or less abundant over time.

One particularly useful technique is mark and recapture. Fish are caught and marked by one of several methods, then released. Later another sample is caught and the proportion of recaptured fish can be used to calculate the number of fish in the entire population. This approach involves many assumptions and we can easily think of factors that might make the results inaccurate. If the fish are not randomly mixed, for instance, the repeat samples may contain disproportionately few or many marked fish. Perhaps the marked fish avoid being caught a second time, or perhaps they are especially vulnerable to capture ("trap happy"). There are lots of reasons for using caution in interpreting mark and recapture data, but often these data are all that fish managers have to base their decisions on.

Ohio, Summer 1966

Sometimes things don't go the way you want them to. In the 1960s I spent several summers teaching ichthyology and fishery biology at the Franz Theodore Stone Laboratory of Ohio State University. The Stone Lab is located on Gibraltar Island in Put-in-Bay, South Bass Island, in Lake Erie. It's a wonderful place to teach because it's right on the water and the streams of northern Ohio are accessible by bus after a short ferry ride to the mainland. Western Lake Erie and its tributary streams have a rich freshwater fish fauna, so it's easy to find material to study and the students are always great—bright, enthusiastic, and captive: the ferry stops running at 8:00 P.M. and the town of Put-in-Bay provides few distractions.

Field courses have to be somewhat flexible to take advantage of special opportunities as they come along. One summer Put-in-Bay was invaded by large numbers of white bass. White bass travel in schools and feed on smaller fish near the surface. Their feeding frenzies can be seen from some distance as they splash and jump at the surface. Once the feeding frenzy starts, very little distracts them, and it's quite easy to row a boat close enough to cast a line into the school. Even an unskilled angler can catch a fish on almost every cast with almost any type of lure.

The arrival of many schools seemed like too good an opportunity to let pass. Since nearly all of the students liked to fish, we set up a special project. The students were to catch all the white bass they could and mark each one by clipping a fin to indicate the part of the bay where it was caught—left pectoral fin for the northwest, right pectoral for the northeast, left pelvic for the southwest, and so on. Fin clipping is a standard marking technique and the fish soon learn to compensate for the missing part. This process would provide two kinds of information when fish were recaptured. Since we could tell where in the bay each fish was first caught, its location when it was recaptured would give us information on movements, and when we got enough recaptures we would be able to estimate the number of white bass in the bay by assuming that the marked and unmarked fish were randomly mixed and therefore the ratio in our last sample would be representative of the entire population in the bay. Since we would know how many fish we had marked and how many were in the sample, simple arithmetic would give us at least a crude estimate of the total number in the bay.

For about a week things went well. The students spent every spare moment catching and marking fish, more than 250 in all. But then we realized we had a problem. We got no recaptures, absolutely none. Either the number of fish in the bay was infinite (a tantalizing notion that we relinquished reluctantly) or the white bass were simply migrating through the bay and didn't remain long enough to be caught a second time. Or could the fish have learned to avoid the lures after being caught once? Or could the fin clipping have put them at a disadvantage, so they were beaten to the lures by intact fish? We're still wondering.

Fish Communities

People are storytellers. They like to weave isolated facts together into some kind of comprehensive narrative. That's why anyone who becomes a fish watcher soon goes beyond observing individual species to try to understand the complex interactions that go on in a pond or stretch of stream. A skilled fish watcher approaches the subjects like the town gossip, gathering isolated facts and building them into a story, then contriving ways to see if the story is really true. Is the grocery clerk deliberately shortchanging his customers or was that an isolated honest mistake? Does the pike selectively feed on shiners or does it simply strike at anything that moves? Do sculpins feed on trout eggs or do they simply take advantage of the few eggs that don't get buried when the female trout covers her nest? Each species has a specific set of habitat requirements. Species whose requirements are similar will naturally be found together. When we find that brook trout and blacknose dace are the only inhabitants of a small cold stream, is it merely because they have the same requirements or is there a deeper relationship, so that if one is removed, the other will also disappear? If there is such a relationship, are the species mutually dependent or is it a one-way relationship, so that the first is dependent on the second but the second can do without the first? Is it possible that some species are dependent on some other species but not necessarily on any one particular species? How do the relationships work? Is it merely that some species provides food for another, or can the situation be more complex, as when one depends on the other to build nests where the eggs of both can be protected?

Ask yourself what effects two species have on each other. Find a stream where two similar species live together and compare their habits. Then find sections of streams where only one of the pair can be found. In the absence of competition, animals tend normally to expand into parts of the habitat that they couldn't use if competitors were present. See if you can find instances of this situation. It was once pointed out to me that mosquitofish keep to the weedy shoreline in pools where predators are present, but that when no predators are about they move freely out into the open areas. Consider resource-sharing mechanisms, such as the time of day when the fish are most active, the kinds and sizes of food they eat, and the shelter sites they occupy. Check out the schools. Are they composed of single species or do different species school together? Which is more important, the species or the size of the individuals? Try to see if you can determine the leading cause of death for several species. Remember that other organisms—birds, amphibians, reptiles, and mammals as well as invertebrates—all play roles in the lives of fishes, and that sometimes small, inconspicuous species provide food or otherwise serve as regulators of species that depend on them at critical times in their life cycle.

Sometimes we can learn a great deal by studying fishes in small, artificial systems such as aquariums and farm ponds. Even a small pond can provide many hours of recreation for anyone lucky enough to own one. A common practice is to stock a pond with bluegills and largemouth bass. The bluegills feed mostly on insects. They are fun to catch and their young are good food for the predatory bass. The possibility of catching a fair-sized bass makes the fishing even more interesting. The hope is to maintain a balance so that both the bass and the bluegills have enough food and grow rapidly to a respectable size. Bluegills, however, can reproduce so rapidly that the bass alone are unable to keep the bluegill population in check, and unless many are removed by fishing, the bluegills may become so abundant that there won't be enough insects for them to feed on. Then they will feed on the bass fry and prevent the bass from reproducing successfully. Furthermore, bluegills will continue to reproduce even when they are starved, and the result is a pond full of undersized but sexually active bluegills. If there are dense weeds in the pond, the bass may be unable to get enough to eat because the bluegills hide in the weeds.

Whether or not a pond remains in balance depends on such factors as its size and shape, the amount of vegetation present, the initial ratio of bass to bluegills, and whether other fish species are present. The management of populations is difficult even in such simple systems, and sooner or later most ponds get out of balance.

We are just beginning to recognize the importance of managing entire communities rather than selectively encouraging the few species we consider important. In the next few years nongame species will assume increasing importance in our management strategies as we learn to cope with the complexity of natural communities. When we attempt to simplify the system by concentrating on only one or two game fishes, we risk upsetting the natural balance and creating an unstable population structure. At present the only technique we have for managing whole communities is to protect the habitat from modification or destruction and otherwise let the plants and animals alone to sort things out by themselves.

As we learn more about fish communities, it becomes apparent that any stability in natural communities is the result of complex interactions about which we know very little. The often ignored smaller organisms play subtle but important and possibly crucial roles in community economics. In the long run, seemingly unimportant organisms may prove to be the key to the management of the commercially and recreationally valued species.

Oklahoma, Summer 1969

Brier Creek is a small tributary of the Red River, or more properly of Lake Texoma, which is a very large impoundment of the Red River. The University of Oklahoma maintains a biological station on Lake Texoma and one summer I was privileged to serve as a visiting professor there. One of the responsibilities of the job was to work with a professor interested in obtaining some additional research experience. Professor Charlie R. Powell and I decided to study the fish communities of Brier Creek. We set up a series of stations along the length of the stream and sampled them every week throughout the summer. We were able to drive to some of the headwater stations, but downstream stations were accessible only by boat. The upstream stations were small and we had to be careful not to deplete the populations; the downstream stations were deep and so full of sunken trees that they were quite difficult to sample. The disparities made it difficult to standardize our samples. The usual practice is to pull the net over the same distance each week, but we found that the net got snagged so often that our results weren't comparable. In the end we settled for collecting until our sample jar contained approximately the same volume of specimens as it had held the week before.

Both lower and upper stations were usually so turbid that we were discouraged from doing much fish watching, but in the mid-reach section of the stream the water was clear. There we could see schools of stonerollers in the pools and the lower reaches of the riffle areas, and we could confirm our identifications by judicious use of the seine, cutting off particular schools to see what kinds of fish they were. This region also had some beautiful large longear sunfish, Lepomis megalotis, *with very large opercular flaps and bright coppery-red breasts.*

The headwaters consisted of isolated pools that got cut off as the summer progressed and the water table dropped. One of the prettiest fishes was the redfin shiner, Cyprinella lutrensis, *a small minnow with bright-red fins.*

Plains streams such as Brier Creek are subject to great seasonal variation, and during the flood times the fish must be severely disturbed and redistributed. One interesting observation was that the common carp, so often a dominant pest, seemed to have fitted into the natural community without noticeably disrupting anything.

Today Dr. William Mathews of the biological station is conducting much more sophisticated studies on Brier Creek, and the creek continues to yield information on how the fishes live together.

How They Got Here

Nearly every body of water of any size in North America has some fish in it. The fishes of North America constitute two distinctive faunas. The western fishes are confined to the area west of the Rocky Mountains, and the eastern fauna occupies the remainder of the continent. Over time many eastern fishes have been introduced into western waters, often to the great detriment of the native species, but historically the faunas were quite distinct. The eastern fauna has several subdivisions, and the ranges of northern and southern species may either be completely separate or overlap to some degree. A few species are limited to the extreme southern part of Florida; some others originally were never found north of Texas.

When you consider the fish of an isolated pond, one of the questions you are sure to ask is "How did the fish get here?" Most ponds have an outlet of some sort, and it is possible for fish to swim to the pond when the flow is high. Some ponds, however, have no outlets, or have outlets with seemingly impassable falls. Besides, fishes that live in small ponds are not likely to spend much time in small, swift streams. Here we must seek a historical explanation of fish distribution.

In many cases the fish were deliberately introduced in the hope that they would provide food or recreation. Some fish may have been introduced thoughtlessly when fishers discarded unused bait or aquarists released unwanted pets.

Still, there are waters where there is reason to believe that the fish have not been introduced and we have to seek a further explanation. One of the most intriguing is the possibility that the species actually were present when the pond was formed, some as long ago as the last ice age, nearly 20,000 years ago. As the ice sheets were melting so that their edges were receding, enormous glacial lakes were formed along their margins. Some fishes were able to move freely through these lakes while others could not because glacial lakes are not very good fish habitats. The pumpkinseed sunfish, brook trout, white and longnose suckers, and a few other species were probably able to do reasonably well in periglacial lakes and were able to travel freely through them. As the glacial outlets changed and as the glacier front got farther away, the large glacial lakes began to shrink and break up into isolated ponds. The fish that were present were then trapped and their descendants still live there today.

Since fishes cannot travel overland, any species that live in the headwater parts of streams are effectively isolated from other populations of the same species that live in other stream drainages, even though they may live only a short distance apart as the crow flies. It is believed that this isolation has been responsible for the evolution of species. Consider the johnny darter and the tessellated darter. These species are closely similar, differing only in such features as the number of rays in the fins. The johnny darter is widely distributed in the Mississippi drainage and the tessellated darter lives in the streams that flow into the Atlantic Ocean. Their similarity strongly suggests that they are descendants of a single species. At some time in the past a barrier formed between the two parts of their range and gradually mutations accumulated in each population until they could no longer interbreed when they came together after the glaciers receded. Did this differentiation occur during the last glacial period or did it happen earlier? Until recently we could only guess at the answers to such questions, but newer genetic techniques may soon give us convincing explanations.

In eastern North America the Appalachian Mountains separate the Atlantic coastal plain from the broad central area drained by the Mississippi River and its tributaries. Today the Great Lakes, the St.

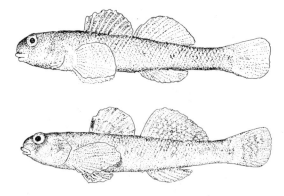

The johnny darter, *Etheostoma nigrum*.

The tessellated darter, *Etheostoma olmstedi*. The johnny darter is widely distributed west of the Appalachian Mountains and the tessellated darter lives along the Atlantic Coast. They come together in the Lake Ontario region.

Lawrence Valley, and, to a lesser extent, the Mohawk corridor connect the two regions, but when the Great Lakes region was covered by ice, the northern Atlantic drainages were quite separated from the Mississippi watershed. As the ice receded, the outlets changed. Water from the region that is now Lake Ontario flowed into the Mississippi during the height of the glaciation, then southeastward through the Susquehanna valleys, then east through the Mohawk-Hudson, and finally northeast through the St. Lawrence River. The fishes that live in the northern states and Canada have repopulated the area since the retreat of the last glacier. They must have come from three major sources—the meltwaters along the edge of the glacier itself, the Mississippi Valley, and the Atlantic Coast drainages.

Because each species of fish has its own particular environmental requirements, the various species did not settle new colonies simultaneously. Those that were able to tolerate the harsh conditions of the glacial meltwaters could move in almost as soon as the ice left the area. Others had to wait until conditions became more suitable, by which time some of the glacial outlets had closed as the flowing meltwaters chose other routes. For such species, the invasion—or, as we suspect in many cases, reinvasion—of the glaciated region was a slow process that depended largely on a sequence of stream captures.

Stream capture is a fascinating geological process. All streams gradually erode the land close to their sources, and adjacent streams from time to time "collide" as they wear away the land between them, with the result that one stream takes over—captures—the upper sections of an adjacent stream. When this happens, any fish that were living in the headwaters suddenly find themselves in an entirely different watershed even though they are still in the same geographic location. Most stream captures occur between tributary streams in the same major drainage so they have relatively little effect on fish distribution, but they do serve to preserve genetic diversity by preventing isolation and inbreeding. Sometimes, however, the results are dramatic, as when the Hudson took the Great Lakes away from the Mississippi River (only to lose out later when the St. Lawrence became free of ice).

Stream captures can be seen on the local level. Look at a map showing stream course. Normally tributaries converge downstream; that is, they form an acute angle on the upstream side of the convergence. But where there has been a stream capture, the tributaries tend to come together so that the acute angle is on the downstream side. The headwaters have a fishhook appearance on the map, and these are, in fact, called barbed tributaries. Good examples are the Wallkill River in the Hudson River drainage and the Maumee River in western Ohio and eastern Indiana.

Once you have found some possible stream capture sites on the map, it is interesting to look at a topographic map to see where passes through the hills indicate the former stream courses. Then you will want to visit the sites to see the evidence for yourself.

Sometimes floods carry fishes from one drainage to another. Beaver dams probably connect the upper parts of some drainages, allowing some species access to new areas.

In the early nineteenth century De Witt Clinton, a naturalist and statesman who is best known for his struggle to get the Erie Canal ("Clinton's Ditch") built, took a trip to the western part of New York State and visited Niagara Falls. He realized that fish couldn't swim up the falls, yet they were abundant in Lake Erie. After he thought about it, he came up with the idea that perhaps they came from the Mississippi during floods through the lowlands south of Lake Michigan, But this explanation didn't seem too likely to him; a better one,

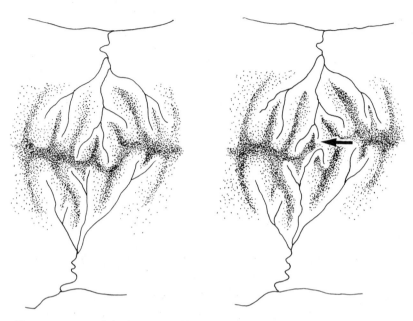

Stream capture and the formation of barbed tributaries (arrow). The middle branch of the stream flowing south has captured the upper reach of the middle branch of the stream flowing north. The upper part of the captured stream still flows north before it turns at the point where it was captured.

he decided, was that they arrived during the biblical flood. As the waters receded and gradually became less salty, he reasoned, the fish were able to adapt to fresh water. Remember that this was nearly a half century before Charles Darwin published his *Origin of Species*. Clinton's concept demonstrates an ingenious blending of his faith in the Bible and insight into the workings of evolution through gradual adaptation. Obviously De Witt Clinton was a perceptive and innovative thinker who knew an interesting problem when he saw one.

Kansas, Summer 1952

In the summer of 1952 I had an opportunity to participate in a field study that confirmed my love of fieldwork in general and gave me a

*new view of the North American fauna. The leader of the trip was the
late Dr. Claude W. Hibbard of the Museum of Paleontology of the
University of Michigan. Earlier in his career Hibbard had discovered
that the sediments of the high plains contained a startling variety of
vertebrate microfossils, the remains of small animals—mice, voles,
skunks, and the like. They had largely been overlooked by earlier
paleontologists, who concentrated on large animals such as horses,
camels, elephants, giant sloths, and beavers, not to mention dino-
saurs. Hibbard recognized that the smaller organisms told as much
about the environmental conditions of the past as the larger animals
did—more, in fact, because there were more of them. From the 1940s
until his death in 1973 Hibbard worked nearly every summer in western Kansas, amassing large collections of small bones and mollusc
shells. Ultimately he was able to find faunas representing all of the
major glacial and interglacial periods. The glacial faunas consisted of
such mammals as bog lemmings, and the interglacial faunas included
southern forms such as cotton rats.*

*Hibbard was one of the most effective college professors I ever knew.
Several of his students are leaders in the field today. He taught by
example. He looked, talked, and chewed tobacco like a Kansas farmer
and he was a whiz at fixing windmills and the hydraulic ram that
supplied the water for our camp. Hydraulic rams are mystical ma-
chines that somehow use the inertia of a flowing stream to pump water
to a higher level. Each stroke lifts about a teaspoonful but the machine
never stops and never needs fuel. The world needs more hydraulic
rams and Hibbards to fix them. Lecturing was never Hibbard's strong
point, but his enthusiasm was unbounded and contagious and his
office door was always open. His voluminous publications represent a
tremendous contribution to paleontology in North America.*

*Hibbard's field technique was to walk the draws (dry creek beds)
looking for places where small bones had washed out of the dirt banks.
When he found a promising spot, he and his crew carefully shoveled
dirt into burlap sacks and gently loaded them on a small truck. Back at
camp we carefully dried the dirt on canvas over wire racks and then
washed it by placing a shovelful at a time in a screen-bottomed box and
setting the box in a small stream that flowed through the state park
that was our headquarters. After the running water had carried the
sediments away, the remaining material was dumped out on weighted
laboratory towels and dried again. The system was pretty well stan-*

dardized. On alternate days we worked in the field, digging and sacking dirt. The other days we washed dirt in the morning and spent the afternoon under a cottonwood tree, picking through the residue for fossils. When we came to something special, such as a mouse jaw or part of a skull, we carefully wrapped it in cigarette paper and added it to the collection of limb bones, isolated teeth, fish scales, and other bone fragments in the Prince Albert tobacco can that was as much a part of our gear as our watch or our hat. The work was hot, dirty, and thoroughly satisfying.

The next year I studied some of the fish remains and eventually published my first serious paper on North American fishes. Among the skeletal remains from the Behrends fauna, which dated back to the time of the Ilinoisan glacial advance, I was able to identify parts of about ten species of fishes, only two of which still live in the area.

When I plotted the present range of each species on a separate base map, then cut that area out of each map and stacked the maps, the resulting hole showed where all of the species occur together now. It turned out that this area is in the Great Lakes region, far to the northeast of the Oklahoma panhandle. This is pretty clear evidence that as the glaciers advanced, the climate south of the glaciated region changed so that the fishes were able to extend their ranges southward into regions where they cannot live today. Not much, perhaps, not even unexpected, but a solid piece in the growing body of knowledge of past history of the fishes of North America.

Humans have had profound effects on the distribution of fishes. One of the first attempts to improve fishing was the importation of exotic species or of species from other parts of the country. These activities are still going on, although they are restricted by law in most areas. A few introductions, such as the importation of the brown trout from Europe and the rainbow trout from the western United States to the East, are generally considered beneficial. The deliberate release of common carp and goldfish, though, is generally thought to be a mild disaster, and the invasion of the upper Great Lakes by sea lampreys through the Welland Canal is a full-scale catastrophe.

The effects of the canals built in the early and mid–nineteenth century are sometimes difficult to determine because the canals were built through the lowest areas between watersheds. These areas are the sites of ancient stream captures or former glacial outlets, so it is hard to tell whether the way the species are distributed can be traced to the canals or to earlier connections. If a species is widespread in one drainage and lives only near a canal in the other, however, we presume that it came through the canal.

A word of warning: The canal-building era is one of the most interesting periods in American history. Canals require large quantities of water but very little additional energy to operate. These canals, constructed before the days of bulldozers and backhoes, are monuments to human industry. Many family histories are connected with the canals in one way or another. Beware of the fascination of tracing canal routes; it can seriously cut into your fish watching.

Nature and People

The past three decades have seen some drastic changes in our attitudes toward the environment. Before 1960 the predominant attitude was that the natural world was created for our use and we were remiss if we failed to harvest what was there to be harvested. Very few people gave any thought to the future. Coal was to be mined, oil and gas were to be pumped, trees to be cut, fish to be caught, deer to be shot. Conservationists, some of them with remarkable achievements to their credit, were to be tolerated as long as they kept their voices low and their demands modest.

Flowing water has an independent spirit; it is not given to following arbitrary human rules. Just to show civilization who is boss, flowing water sometimes comes into direct conflict with humanity's best interests by washing out roads, undermining building erected too close to watercourse, and general flooding. In retaliation, engineers have channeled and rerouted streams, built dams to control flooding, and constructed canals to join waterways where nature failed to do so. Part of the need for these measures was civilization's fault in the first place. As the forests were cleared, the land could no longer absorb the rainfall as it came down, and the results were flooding and, later, excessive drying. In densely forested regions the water is soaked up as it falls and then released slowly so that stream flow is maintained without drastic changes throughout the year.

In another way, though, the rivers have outsmarted themselves. Because of the general cussedness of flowing waters, people came to regard them as invincible, so it didn't seem to matter what was done to our waterways. Streams were and in some places still are used as sewers and garbage dumps in full confidence that they could handle anything we chose to throw in them. They were great places to throw construction debris, old automobiles, and shopping carts. They were rumored to have a special appetite for noxious chemical wastes, worn-out metal-plating solutions, paints, old motor oil, surplus pesticides, and anything else that people no longer had a use for.

The streams tried. For a century or so after the Europeans arrived, they took everything we gave them, but eventually it got to be too much and the waters began to lose the battle. Sometimes they flooded just to get rid of the debris. Often this tactic worked, but when it comes to trash, the forces of natural degradation can never compete with the human species. With the advent of synthetic chemicals the streams had no chance. They are not dead and they can still recover to some extent, but now they need a lot of help. Even under the best of conditions the restored streams will never be exactly like the originals.

The value of wetlands is especially difficult for many people to comprehend. You can't plow them and you can't build on them. They don't grow timber and you can't water-ski on them. But they do make wonderful dumps. As a result of this attitude, many wetlands have been annihilated—drained for agriculture, filled for building, sacrificed for "sanitary" landfills. Unlike some of the pollution of streams and even lakes, these losses are forever.

What have we lost? What good are wetlands? For some people their beauty alone justifies their preservation. We also know that wetlands are valuable as habitat for wildfowl and other wildlife and as nursery grounds for fishes. They are also inexpensive and very practical water reservoirs, soaking up rainfall in the spring and releasing it during the dry months of summer, purifying the water as they maintain the flow of streams.

Marshes can also do much of the final processing of our sewage, converting nutrients into plant material by using only their own organic machinery and solar energy. An existing swamp is a far lesser tax burden than a tertiary treatment plant. But it takes longer to build a swamp than to dig a sewer.

And then the tide turned. We suddenly became aware that we are running out of nonrenewable resources and at the same time we realized that the quality of our own environment had deteriorated to an unacceptable degree. A growing number of people banded together to advance the ecological movement and politicians suddenly found it in their interests to pass legislation intended to protect our environment and improve the quality of life. Endangered species were singled out and stringent protective measures were enacted. Pollution abatement was given high priority, and the more developed nations banned such uncontrollable substances as DDT and PCBs. Nuclear power plants, with their unsolved waste problems, were opposed with increasing fervor. Suddenly our society became polarized between the "no nukes" and the "pro-nukes." The choices are difficult because there is no easy way to balance risks against costs and benefits, especially when some of the benefits are as intangible as "quality of life."

Some of the legislation that purports to protect our environment has been less than perfect. Some measures have placed impossible burdens on our industries and have forced them into alternatives that are worse than the problems they were designed to avoid. Some have diverted our energies away from the solution of real problems and have made it difficult or impossible to gather the knowledge needed to develop rational practices and intelligent policies. Many good laws are not being enforced for lack of resources or for political reasons. And, saddest of all, some laws that proved to be burdensome have been abandoned rather than modified to practical levels, thus causing reversals that have undone much hard-won progress.

The environmental concerns that have plagued our civilization for decades have no simple solutions. We need energy and materials to survive and we produce wastes. We are running out of resources and our wastes are overwhelming us. In our efforts to find solutions we have often displayed the human tendency to go too far in everything we do. In the years to come we can expect periods of unacceptably restrictive protectionist legislation to alternate with periods of unconscionable laxity. It is going to be a long war.

During the lulls in the ecological battle, when the warriors fall back to regroup and there is time to contemplate what it really is we are fighting for, let us enjoy watching the fish.

A glass-bottom "view box," sometimes called a water telescope, is useful for watching lampreys on their nest.

Fishes can be seen clearly in the still water next to a bulkhead.

Even in this slightly turbid midwestern stream the shadows of a school of minnows can be seen on the bottom.

A polarizing filter removes surface reflections. Looking into a stream (top) without the filter and (bottom) with the filter.

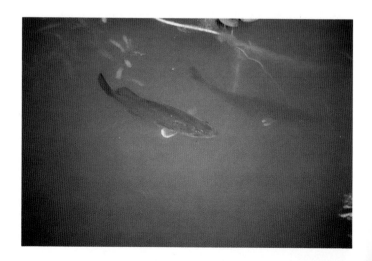

Smallmouth bass cruise near a weed bed.

Banded killifish feed near the surface.

A piece of discarded lumber provides a nest for a male fathead minnow.

In a small pond a sunfish has built its nest next to a boulder outcrop.

Rocky headwaters.

A base-level stream
flows through the
Basherkill Wildlife
Management Area
in southeastern
New York State.

Swamps are
wooded wetlands.

A northern pond with mats of vegetation along its edge.

This Michigan lake has a sandy ledge along the shore where logperch and trout-perch spawn during the summer.

Old tree stumps provide excellent cover for fishes.

Beds of submerged aquatic vegetation are nursery and shelter areas.

On very cold nights stream water can be cooled below freezing. Ice crystals can then form flocculent "anchor ice."

Sometimes the anchor ice displaces the stream water during the night, leaving surface ice attached to the shore well above the normal stream level.

Sea lamprey,
Petromyzon marinus,
on its nest.

Ohio lamprey,
Ichthyomyzon bdellium,
and its host, a river chub,
Nocomis micropogon.

Breeding male
common shiner,
Luxilus cornutus.

The breeding colors
of the longnose dace,
Rhinichthys cataractae.

The introduced goldfish,
Carassius auratus, is
now widespread in
North America.

Male brown trout
develop hooked lower
jaws as they mature.

Sculpins are
bottom-dwelling fishes.
(Photo by Raymond A. Mendez.)

The variegate darter,
Etheostoma variatum, is
one of the more colorful
stream-dwelling darters.
(Photo by Raymond A. Mendez.)

Johnny darters,
Etheostoma nigrum,
often live in slow
waters and even in
lakes and ponds.
They lack the brilliant
colors of many darters.
(Photo by Raymond A. Mendez.)

Male greenside darters,
Etheostoma blennioides,
are extremely colorful in
the breeding season.

Goldfish spawning
in a small pond.

Logperch,
Percina caprodes,
spawning in the
sandy shallows of a
small lake in Michigan.

Swarms of baby bullheads, *Ameiurus nebulosus,* form black clouds in the shallows of Lake Michigan.

A pebble nest, probably built by a fallfish, *Semotilus corporalis,* has been exposed by the falling water level. The beverage can serves as a scale.

A male sunfish, *Lepomis auritus,* guarding its nest in an Adirondack lake.

Eggs of a fathead minnow, *Pimephales promelas,* deposited on the underside of a piece of wood. These eggs are guarded by the male, who grooms them with a fleshy pad in front of his dorsal fin.

A male fathead minnow displays breeding tubercles and a fleshy pad behind the head.

Eggs of a fantail darter, *Etheostoma flabellare,* laid on the underside of a flat rock. The male guards the eggs and grooms them with the expanded fleshy tips of his dorsal spines.

6   For More Information

The literature dealing with fishes is widely scattered and much of it is rather technical. Here are a few books that will help you get started.

GENERAL REFERENCES

Boyle, Robert H. 1979. *The Hudson River: A Natural and Unnatural History.* New York: Norton. 325 pp. A marvelously passionate account of the Hudson, its people, and its problems. Lots of good natural history.

Breder, Charles M., Jr., and Donn Eric Rosen. 1966. *Modes of Reproduction in Fishes.* Neptune City, N.J.: TFH. 941 pp. A thorough compendium of the reproductive processes in fishes. A wonderful resource book.

Cole, John N. 1978. *Striper: A Story of Fish and Man.* Boston: Little, Brown/ Atlantic Monthly Press. 269 pp. The story of the Long Island commercial fishery for striped bass.

Curtis, Brian. 1971. *The Life History of the Fish: His Manners and Morals.* Reprint of 1949 rev. ed. New York: Dover. 248 pp.

Hay, John. 1959. *The Run.* Garden City, N.Y.: Doubleday. 189 pp. A delightful account of alewife spawning and its place in New England history.

Moyle, Peter B., and Joseph J. Cech, Jr. 1988. *Fishes: An Introduction to Ichthyology.* 2d ed. Englewood Cliffs, N.J.: Prentice-Hall. 559 pp. An excellent introductory textbook. Easy reading and lots of information.

Nelson, Joseph S. 1984. *Fishes of the World.* 2d ed. New York: Wiley. 523 pp. A technical listing of fish families. Concise and informative, this book summarizes the current knowledge of the world's fishes. Excellent for the serious student and a useful adjunct for the serious fish watcher. Helps to put things in perspective.

Norman, J. R., and P. H. Greenwood. 1975. *A History of Fishes*. 3d ed. New York: Wiley. An excellent introduction to fishes, not too technical, containing a wealth of material. A standard for the beginner.

Wilson, Roberta, and James Q. Wilson. 1985. *Watching Fishes: Life and Behavior on Coral Reefs*. New York: Harper & Row. 275 pp. An excellent guide to the natural history of coral reef fishes. Lots of good ideas for the dryland fish watcher.

REGIONAL GUIDES

Becker, George C. 1983. *Fishes of Wisconsin*. Madison: University of Wisconsin Press. 1052 pp. A huge compilation of what is known about the fishes of Wisconsin. Tremendous amount of natural history information. An incredible book!

Cooper, Edwin L. 1983. *Fishes of Pennsylvania and the Northeastern United States*. University Park: Pennsylvania State University Press. 243 pp. Another regional guide with very good black-and-white photographs.

Hubbs, Carl L., and Karl F. Lagler. 1974. *Fishes of the Great Lakes Region*. Ann Arbor: University of Michigan Press. 213 pp. One of the best regional fish books ever published. Emphasizes identification and distribution. A perennial classic.

Morrow, James E. 1980. *The Freshwater Fishes of Alaska*. Anchorage: Alaska Northwest. 248 pp. Has some exquisite illustrations.

Page, Lawrence M., and Brooks, M. Burr. 1991. *A Field Guide to Freshwater Fishes, North America North of Mexico*. Peterson Field Guide Series. Boston: Houghton Mifflin. 432 pp. Just what the fish watcher ordered!

Pflieger, William L. 1975. *The Fishes of Missouri*. Jefferson City: Missouri Department of Conservation. 342 pp. Superbly designed and illustrated regional handbook. One of the best.

Robison, Henry W., and Thomas M. Buchanan. 1988. *Fishes of Arkansas*. Fayetteville: University of Arkansas Press. 536 pp. Excellent.

Scarola, John F. 1973. *Freshwater Fishes of New Hampshire*. Concord: New Hampshire Fish and Game Department. 131 pp. Has some excellent color photographs.

Scott, W. B., and E. J. Crossman. 1973. *Freshwater Fishes of Canada*. Fisheries Research Board of Canada Bulletin 184. 966 pp. A first-rate compendium of the fishes of Canada and what is known about them. Remarkable for its thoroughness.

Smith, C. Lavett. 1986. *The Inland Fishes of New York State*. Albany: New York State Department of Environmental Conservation. 523 pp. A guide to fishes of the state, with summaries of life history, distribution, and nomenclature.

Smith, Philip W. 1979. *The Fishes of Illinois*. Urbana: University of Illinois Press. 314 pp. Another excellent and well-designed regional fish book.

Tomelleri, Joseph R., and Mark E. Eberle. 1990. *Fishes of the Central United States.* Lawrence: University Press of Kansas. 226 pp. Features Tomelleri's beautiful and precise paintings.

Trautman, Milton B. 1981. *The Fishes of Ohio with Illustrated Keys.* Rev. ed. Columbus: Ohio State University Press. 782 pp. This superb compilation emphasizes the changes that have taken places since Ohio was settled. Excellent for identifying fishes from the Great Lakes and Ohio River drainages.

Whitworth, Walter R., Peter L. Berrien, and Walter T. Keller. 1968. *Freshwater Fishes of Connecticut.* Bulletin 101, State Geological and Natural History Survey of Connecticut. 134 pp. Guide to the fishes of southern New England.

These are only a few of the available guides to fishes in the eastern United States. Most states also publish smaller guides to sport fishes and more technical reports.

Along the coast you will find the following books useful, and they are also good for looking up some of the fishes that you find in your local fish market:

Bigelow, Henry B., and W. C. Schroeder. 1953. *Fishes of the Gulf of Maine.* Fishery Bulletin 74, U.S. Fish and Wildlife Service. 577 pp. The classic and still all-around best reference for fishes of the northeastern Atlantic Coast states.

Roberts, Mervin F. 1985. *The Tidemarsh Guide to Fishes.* Old Saybrook, Conn.: Saybrook Press. 373 pp. An excellent guide arranged by fish shapes. Sized to be used in the field.

Robins, C. Richard, and G. Carleton Ray. 1986. *A Field Guide to the Atlantic Coast Fishes of North America.* Peterson Field Guide Series. Boston: Houghton Mifflin. 354 pp. This book emphasizes identification and distribution of marine fishes. An excellent job by two very competent ichthyologists. Another book in the series covers the Pacific Coast fishes.

SELECTED FAMILIES

Both of these excellent and comprehensive books on our most colorful freshwater fishes are illustrated with beautiful color photographs:

Kuehne, Robert A., and Roger W. Barbour. 1983. *The American Darters.* Louisville: University of Kentucky Press. 177 pp.

Page, Lawrence M. 1983. *Handbook of Darters.* Neptune City, N.J.: TFH. 271 pp.

KEEPING FISHES

More and more aquarists are developing an interest in North American freshwater fishes:

Quinn, John R. 1990. *Our Native Fishes: The Aquarium Hobbyist's Guide to Observing, Collecting, and Keeping Them.* Woodstock, Vt.: Countryman Press. 241 pp.

DISTRIBUTION

For a serious study of fish distribution, these two sources are essential:

Hocutt, Charles H., and E. O. Wiley, eds. 1986. *The Zoogeography of North American Freshwater Fishes.* New York: Wiley. 866 pp.
Lee, David, et al. 1980–. *Atlas of North American Freshwater Fishes.* Raleigh: North Carolina State Museum of Natural History. 854 pp. Periodic supplements. Supplement 1983, 67 pp.

NAMES OF FISHES

And if you should get interested in scientific names and their meanings, try these two:

Brown, Roland Wilbur. 1956. *Composition of Scientific Words.* Washington, D.C.: Smithsonian Institution Press. 882 pp.
Jaeger, Edmund C. 1950. *A Source-Book of Biological Names and Terms.* Springfield, Ill.: Charles C Thomas. 287 pp.

The Classification of Fishes

Modern Classification

Before we go any further let us stop and consider what fishes are. Broadly defined, they are vertebrate animals that in adulthood breathe by means of gills and swim by means of fins. This definition serves reasonably well in everyday use. It certainly distinguishes fish from birds, reptiles, and mammals. Modern biologists, however, find it quite inadequate because it turns out that a careful analysis of the structure of fishes reveals that some groups of fishes differ far more from each other than birds do from mammals. Moreover, crocodiles are closer to birds than to other groups of reptiles, and mammals, including you and me, are closer to herrings than we are to lampreys, even though both lampreys and herrings have gills and fins and we don't.

Here's how it works. All of the first vertebrates had gills of some kind. Some modern vertebrates have lost their gills in the adult stage but they still have them, or at least a trace of them, while they are embryos. This fact indicates that gills are a *primitive* feature common to all vertebrates, and therefore tell us very little about the relationships of the various groups of vertebrates. Fur and mammary glands are unique to mammals. Since they are not present in primitive groups, they are *derived,* or specialized, characters. Their presence in all mammals is evidence that all mammals had a common ancestor with fur and mammary glands. Such shared derived characters are the only indicators of common ancestry.

When we try to classify organisms on the basis of overall similarity, we automatically include both derived and primitive characters and can easily arrive at some very wrong conclusions; as when we grouped lampreys with bony fishes. Lampreys are very primitive vertebrates. Their lack of jaws, primitive fins, and multiple gill slits are all primitive characters. Their parasitic lifestyle, however, is unique to lampreys and unites them as a group. Jaws are derived features that unite all vertebrates except the lampreys and the even more primitive hagfishes. Thus a mammal with jaws is closer to a higher, jawed fish than either is to a lamprey. The conventional concept of a fish is the result of the artificial exclusion of the land-dwelling vertebrates.

A game that teachers sometimes use to help children develop memory skills is "I'm going on a trip." The first person says, "I'm going on a trip and I'm going to take a suitcase." The next person says, "I'm going on a trip and I'm going to take a suitcase and a comb." The next persons says, "I'm going on a trip and I'm going to take a suitcase, a comb, and a toothbrush." And so on. Each person repeats the items the previous players mentioned and adds one more. So it is with the phylogenetic tree. At each step something new is added, and all of the groups beyond that point are united by the presence of the additional specialized characters. The addition of new features can be summarized in a branching diagram called a cladogram.

We cannot classify two groups of anything; all we can do is determine that they are different. With three or more groups, however, we may find shared characteristics that indicate that two are closer to each other than either is to the third. This approach can be continued to provide a classification that tells us what similarities link the various entities, and gives an indication of what their ancestor must have been like.

Relationships between groups of organisms are best illustrated by means of branching diagrams. In essence these diagrams summarize the sequence in which distinctive unifying characters appeared,

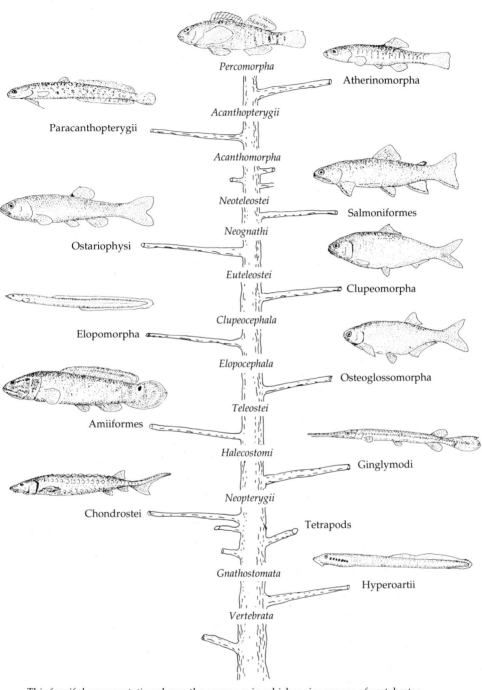

Percomorpha

Atherinomorpha

Acanthopterygii

Paracanthopterygii

Acanthomorpha

Salmoniformes

Neoteleostei

Neognathi

Ostariophysi

Euteleostei

Clupeomorpha

Elopomorpha

Clupeocephala

Elopocephala

Osteoglossomorpha

Teleostei

Amiiformes

Halecostomi

Ginglymodi

Neopterygii

Chondrostei

Tetrapods

Gnathostomata

Hyperoartii

Vertebrata

This fanciful representation shows the sequence in which major groups of vertebrates diverged. The names in italics on the trunk include all of the groups above that point. The Gnathostomata, for example, include all of the groups above the lampreys; the Teleostei include all of the fishes above the Amiiformes. The short, unnamed branches are major fish groups that are not part of our fauna. Notice that the tetrapods branch off the main trunk after the lampreys.

and thus indicate which groups must have had common ancestors. It is these common ancestors that define the closeness of relationships. Consider the relationships of the lampreys, sturgeons, trouts, and sunfishes. All of these fishes must have had a common ancestor that had a backbone and gills. Next we determine the features of each group. Then we construct a diagram indicating which groups have added specialized characteristics. For example, we infer that sturgeons, trouts, and sunfishes (all with jaws) had a common ancestor that was not shared by lampreys, that trouts and sunfishes with modern fins had a common ancestor not shared by sturgeons, and that sunfishes, with true fin spines, had a common ancestor not shared by trout. The last step is to put these deductions together into a scheme of classification:

Vertebrata	Teleostei
Lampreys	Salmoniformes
Gnathostomata	Trouts
Chrondrostei	Percomorpha
Sturgeons	Sunfishes

This way of looking at classification, which has been popular only since the 1960s, has changed our ideas about the way the various families of fishes are related. No classification, however, is ever considered final. Zoologists continue to study animals in search of more shared derived characters that will confirm or refute the present classifications, or permit us to refine our current understandings.

Recently some zoologists have turned to biochemical techniques, such as studies of enzymes and DNA sequencing in their search for shared derived characters that will help them clarify relationships. Sophisticated computer programs are now used to create the cladograms that require the fewest assumptions. The science of classification of organisms is very much alive.

Many of the features used in the classification of fishes are technical details of anatomy or physiology and beyond the scope of this book. Therefore I have selected one or two of the most obvious and clear-cut markers for each of the higher levels and, following the analogy of the memory game, listed them to indicate where each advanced characteristic first appears. Unless it has been secondarily lost, each addition is present in all of the more advanced groups (those that follow) but in none of the more primitive groups. Specialized features that distinguish the individual branches of the tree are also given.

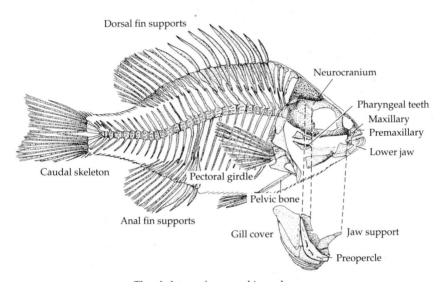

The skeleton of a pumpkinseed.

A diagram of the skeleton of a fairly advanced fish (the pumpkinseed sunfish) will serve for orientation. The following are some of the characteristics used in preparing the phylogenetic tree on page 187:

- The absence of jaws (lampreys) is more primitive than the presence of jaws (all other fishes).
- Fins with spines (perches) are more specialized than fins with only soft rays (trouts). Some groups, however, have secondarily lost their spines (killifishes).
- Pectoral fins with horizontal bases that are low on the side of the body (minnows) are more primitive than pectoral fins with vertical bases that are high on the side of the body (basses).

- Pelvic fins far back on the belly (pikes) are more primitive than those farther forward and attached to the pectoral girdle (sculpins).
- Heterocercal tails with the end of the backbone turned upward (sturgeons) are more primitive than symmetrical tails (herrings).
- Scales that are smooth (herrings) are more primitive than scales that are rough to the touch (sunfishes).
- The absence of scales (catfishes) is a specialization.
- A mouth at the front of the head (trouts) is more primitive than the specialized downturned mouth of suckers or the upturned mouth of killifishes.

These are only a few of the many characteristics used to classify fishes. Sometimes character trends are reversed, as in the case of the fin spines, and sometimes similar features are developed independently in unrelated groups. For this reason zoologists try to identify as many distinguishing features (characters) as they can.

Higher Classification

The tree shown here is a metaphor. Evolution has proceeded as a series of divergences, or branchings. Since trees grow in somewhat the same way, it seems natural to call our branching diagrams trees. In the formal scientific literature branching diagrams are rigorously stylized to avoid the impression that they carry any information other than the sequences of the divergences. Here perhaps we can be permitted to carry the metaphor a little further.

A close look at the diagram of relationships (technically, a clado-gram) on page 187 reveals that the tree is formed by a series of simple dichotomous branchings. The trunk continues upward and the smaller single branch goes off to the side. The implication is that the branches farther up the trunk are more closely related to each other than to the diverging branch. Sometimes we simply do not have enough information to determine which branches are most closely related; in this situation we let three or more branches come from the same point (as in the tree on p. 87). Multiple branches diverging at the same point are indications of the gaps in our knowledge that indicate where more research is needed. We do not yet know how the families of perciform fishes are related.

As this tree is set up, each branching point produces two branches, one of which leads to a single terminal group while the other (the "trunk") continues on to give rise to additional groups. Terminal groups themselves may, of course, have subbranches. New features that are added to the continuing branch are found in all of the groups beyond that point (unless they have been secondarily lost). As in the children's game, the new features are added to the characteristics of the lower groups. Features of the terminating branches, however, are confined to that branch (and its subbranches).

CRANIATA. All of the organisms we call fishes are craniates; that is, they have a skull, a dorsal hollow nerve cord, and several other technical characteristics. The first branch of the craniata (indicated by a short branch with no name attached) consists of the hagfishes. As they are marine forms, they are not considered here.

VERTEBRATA. All craniates except the hagfishes have a notochord, a skull, and two pairs of semicircular canals in the ear. They also have dorsal, anal, and caudal fins. The hagfishes have only one pair of semicircular canals.

LAMPREYS, HYPEROARTII. Lampreys lack jaws, as do the hagfishes, but their auditory and immune systems are similar to those of the rest of the vertebrates. Thus lampreys and jawed fishes are closer to each other than either is to the hagfishes. The name Hyperoartii comes from the Greek *hyper,* above or very, and *artios,* even-numbered or fitting. It refers to the symmetrical pairs of gills.

The lamprey, *Lampetra appendix,* has multiple symmetrical gill openings.

GNATHOSTOMATA. All of the rest of the vertebrates have developed jaws and paired fins. Here the cladogram shows three short branches. The first represents the cartilaginous fishes, the sharks and rays; the second, the tetrapods or land-dwelling vertebrates; and the third, the African reed-fishes—all very fascinating but outside of our present interests. All of the rest of the fishes in our fauna are bony fishes (Osteichthyes) with advanced fin structure (Actinopterygii).

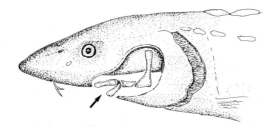

The shortnose sturgeon has jaws.

CHONDROSTEI. The next branch consists of the sturgeons. They have a lot of cartilage in their skeletons and their fins resemble those of sharks, with numerous fine keratinous (horny) rays that are much more numerous than the underlying cartilaginous supports. The tail is strongly heterocercal (asymmetrical with the spinal column turned up to support the dorsal part of the fin).

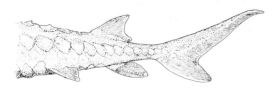

The Atlantic sturgeon, *Acipenser oxyrhynchus*, has numerous fin rays and a heterocercal tail.

NEOPTERYGII. The main line continues, with the remaining groups characterized by modern fins that have bony rays approximately equal in number to the underlying bony supports.

GINGLYMODI. This branch encompasses the gars and their fossil relatives. Gars have premaxillary and maxillary bones associated

The fin rays of the sturgeon (*a*) are fine and numerous. Those of the herring (*b*) are bony and well separated, and most have a separate underlying support.

The longnose gar, *Lepisosteus osseus*, has distinctive ganoid scales and a slightly upturned (abbreviate heterocercal) tail.

with the upper jaw, but these bones are rigidly attached to the skull. In gars the maxillary is divided into several segments, but the segmentation is a specialization.

HALECOSTOMI. The main branch has now added the feature of mobile upper jawbones.

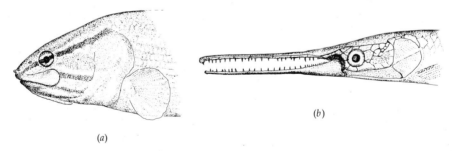

The maxillary bone (upper jaw) of the bowfin (*a*) is movable. In the longnose gar (*b*) the maxillary bone is rigidly attached to the skull.

AMIIFORMES. This branch contains only a single living species, the bowfin. Like the gars, the bowfin has an abbreviate heterocercal tail in which the backbone turns upward, but the tail itself is nearly

The bowfin, *Amia calva*, has an abbreviate heterocercal tail.

symmetrical. The bowfin and its fossil relatives are united by a specialized joint at the hinge of the lower jaw.

TELEOSTEI. From this point on all groups have a specialized type of caudal fin skeleton in which the fin rays are supported by flattened and modified bones called hypurals. The result is an externally symmetrical tail.

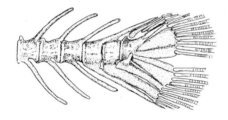

The teleost fishes have homocercal tails supported by flattened hypural plates.

OSTEOGLOSSOMORPHA. This group is represented in North America only by the family Hiodontidae, but there are several other families in the southern hemisphere. The common name bony tongue comes from the fact that the primary bite is between the tongue and a tooth patch in the middle of the roof of the mouth.

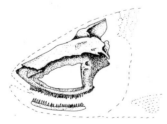

In Osteoglossomorph fishes, represented by the mooneye, *Hiodon tergisus*, the primary bite is between the central keel of the skull and the tongue.

ELOPOCEPHALA. All of the rest of the fishes have riblike epipleural intermuscular bones attached to the pleural ribs and the anterior

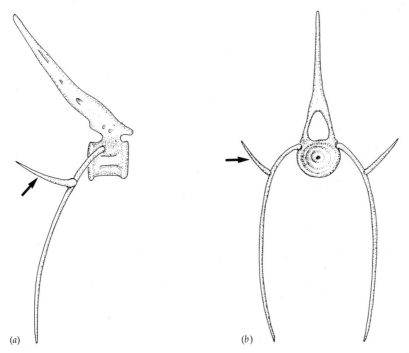

(*a*)　　　　　　　　　　　　　(*b*)

The vertebrae of an Elopocephalan have epipleural ribs. (*a*) Lateral view. (*b*) Anterior view.

caudal vertebrae. They also have two distinctive pairs of uroneural bones in the caudal region.

ELOPOMORPHA. The only member of this group in our fauna is the American eel, *Anguilla rostrata*. Elopomorphs include the well-known marine game fishes tarpon and bonefish as well as the true eels. They are united by their extremely specialized leptocephalus larvae.

Elopomorph fishes have a specialized larva called a leptocephalus. This is the leptocephalus of the American eel.

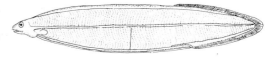

CLUPEOCEPHALA. At this point in the main line the bones of the posterior part of the lower jaw assume their modern form, with a

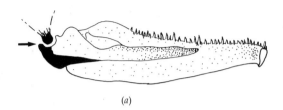

(a)

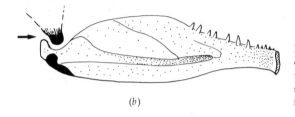

In "lower" fishes such as the moon-eye (a) two bones form the joint of the lower jaw. In advanced fishes such as the smelt (b) only one bone is involved.

(b)

single bone providing the hinge joint that connects the jaw to the skull.

CLUPEOMORPHA. This rather closely knit group is defined by several distinctive features of the skull. Herrings and their close allies are usually schooling silvery fishes with abdominal scutes, specialized head canals, and a diverticulum of the swim bladder connecting with the ear.

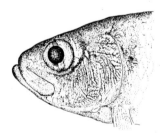

Herrings are characterized by a special arrangement of the sensory canals of the head.

EUTELEOSTEI. The "true" teleosts. Here the characteristics of the main stem of fish evolution are augmented by two more features. First is an adipose fin, which occurs in none of the more primitive groups and is scattered among the advanced fishes. The second is

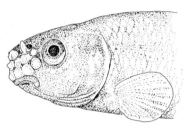

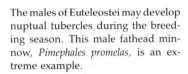

The males of Euteleostei may develop nuptial tubercles during the breeding season. This male fathead minnow, *Pimephales promelas,* is an extreme example.

the presence of breeding tubercles, special skin structures that play a role in reproduction. These have also been lost in some higher groups.

OSTARIOPHYSI. Catfishes, minnows, suckers, and characins make up another lineage that is well defined by the presence of a Weberian apparatus—modifications of the anterior vertebrae including a chin of small bones connecting the swim bladder with the inner ear. The Weberian apparatus apparently endows them with keen hearing. Goldfish, for example, can hear sounds in the range of 40,000 Hz. Ostariophysans dominate the fresh waters of the world but there are only a few truly saltwater ostariophysans. Minnows, suckers, and the Eurasian loaches are the most abundant fishes in the northern hemisphere, and catfishes and characins (many of which are cultivated as aquarium pets) rule the fresh waters of the southern hemisphere (except Australia). South America is also home to the knife fishes and the electric eel, which are also ostariophysans.

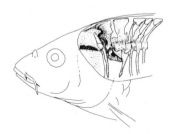

The Weberian apparatus of the carp, *Cyprinus carpio.*

NEOGNATHI. The next innovation of the main line is a modification of the back of the skull so that three bones articulate with the ante-

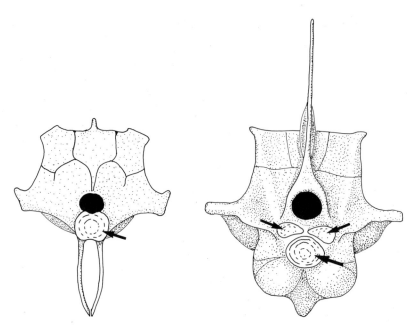

In the Neognathi three bones at the rear of the skull contact the first vertebra, as in the perch (right). In the alewife (left) there is only one contact surface.

rior face of the first vertebra. Up to this point only one bone, the basioccipital, meets the vertebral column.

SALMONIFORMES. Debate continues as to what fishes should be grouped here. Some authorities exclude the smelts and the pikes, essentially leaving only the salmons and trouts.

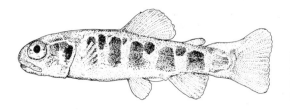

Juvenile trouts, such as this brook trout, *Salvelinus fontinalis*, have well-developed adipose fins and characteristic blotches called parr marks.

NEOTELEOSTEI. With the "new teleosts" the main branch gains an important characteristic, a group of muscles that run from the ver-

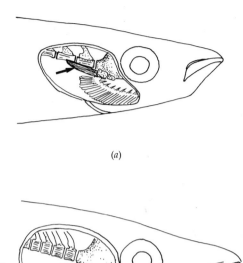

(a)

The Neoteleostei are characterized by the presence of a special muscle to pull the gill arches backward. The retractor muscle is present in the inland silverside, *Menidia beryllina* (*a*), but not in the brook trout, *Salvelinus fontinalis* (*b*).

(b)

tebral column to the upper bones of the gill arches. These muscles make possible more manipulation and grinding of food. You can sometimes see them when you clean your fish for cooking.

At this point three groups of deep-sea fishes, the Stomiiformes, the Aulopiformes, and the Myctophiformes or lanternfishes, diverge. Since they do not occur in North American fresh waters, they will not be discussed further.

ACANTHOMORPHA. After the spitting off of the three deep-sea groups, the remainder of the main line is characterized by four rather technical characters of the skull and its ligaments and also by the presence of well-developed ascending and maxillary processes on the premaxillary bone. Some lower groups have modified fin rays that are spinelike, but true fin spines appear here for the first time. Some acanthomorphs have secondarily lost their spines.

The Acanthomorpha have well-developed ascending and maxillary processes on the premaxillary bone.

PARACANTHOPTERYGII. Opinions differ as to the composition and even the validity of this group. The opercular bone is reduced and the subopercҚulum enlarged, and the caudal skeleton is unique in having only two free epural bones, with the third, anteriormost one fused to the second preural centrum.

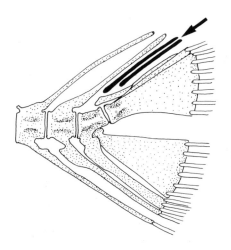

The paracanthopterygian fishes, represented here by the caudal skeleton of the pirate perch, *Aphredoderus sayanus,* are united by having the anteriormost epural bone fused to the next-to-last preural centrum. Most acanthopterygians have three free epural bones.

ACANTHOPTERYGII. At this point the remaining groups are united by the presence of strong spines in the dorsal, anal, and pelvic fins. The premaxillary of acanthopterygian fishes is capable of downward and forward movement, and the retractor dorsalis inserts only on the third pharyngobranchials.

ATHERINOMORPHA. These are spiny rayed fishes, although the spines have been secondarily lost in the killifishes and livebearers. Several features of the jaws and gill arches are unique. The most

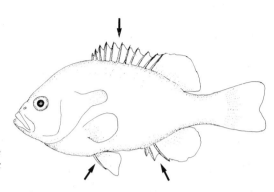

Acanthopterygian fishes have true spines in the dorsal, anal, and pelvic fins.

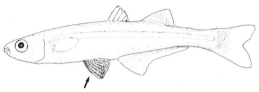

In Atherinomorph fishes the pelvics are located well back on the abdomen and not attached to the pectoral girdle.

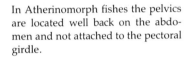

obvious difference between atherinomorphs and percomorphs is that the pelvic fins are far back and not connected to the pectoral girdle in the atherinomorphs.

PERCOMORPHA. This vast group of spiny rayed fishes is poorly understood. At present there is no consensus as to how the included groups are related. All perciforms, however, have the pelvic bones far forward and attached to the pectoral girdles, either directly or by ligaments.

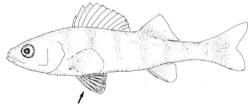

Percomorph fishes have thoracic pelvic fins with the pelvic bones attached to the pectoral girdle.

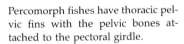

The Scientific Names of Fishes

Bird watchers rarely use scientific names. The common names of birds are well established and widely accepted and there is little chance for confusion. Fish names, unfortunately, are not so stable. The American Society of Ichthyologists and Herpetologists and the American Fisheries Society jointly publish an official list of common and scientific names, but many other names are still in use. Sports writers are doing their best to standardize common names, but the largemouth bass is a green trout throughout much of the South and will be for some time to come. Those of us who are interested in species that aren't widely known find that scientific names are actually easier to use.

For some reason many naturalists and even some professional biologists are afraid of scientific names. Some people are intimidated by the lengths of the words and have trouble pronouncing them. But if you don't use a word, you don't remember it. Botanists and gardeners seem immune to these problems. Nobody gives a second thought to such names as gardenia, azalea, geranium, and coreopsis. This is the way it should be with fish names.

Part of the problem is that many natural history books give short shrift to scientific names. They may explain that the scientific name consists of two words: the name of the genus, which is always capitalized, and the name of the species, which is not. This formulation doesn't really help much. It completely hides the fact that scientific nomenclature is one area where the personalities of the early naturalists show through. Some scientific names tell something about the organisms; others reveal more about the describer.

Consider descriptive names. The species name *atromaculatus* refers to the fact that the creek chub has a black (*ater*) spot (*macula*) at the base of the dorsal fin. *Cornutus*, the trivial (species) name of the common shiner, means "horned"; it refers to the breeding tubercles that develop on the heads of breeding males. Most of the year it would be hard to make the connection, but in the spring the source of the name becomes obvious. *Vitreum*, glassy, certainly describes the eye of the walleye. The list goes on and on. These names really help us when we are learning to recognize the fish and they reveal a lot about how the early naturalists saw the species as they discovered them for the first time.

Some names tell about habits or geographic homelands. The brook trout, for example, is named *fontinalis*, which means "of the spring," and certainly the brook trout is most at home in clear spring-fed streams. The name of the sauger, *canadense*, refers to its Canadian homeland.

Other names honor people. Many of these patronyms, as they are called, celebrate outstanding naturalists. *Bairdii*, for instance, honors Spencer Fullerton Baird, the first U.S. Commissioner of Fisheries. The spoonhead sculpin, *Cottus ricei*, was named for the person who collected the first specimen. Some naturalists named new species for their wives or for assistants who rendered exceptional services.

Scientific names are applied in accordance with the *International Code of Zoological Nomenclature*. These rules are somewhat complex but they are fun to read. English and French versions appear on facing pages because the International Commission on Zoological Nomenclature could not agree on which language to use. Remember that the commission is concerned only with names, not with whether species and genera are actually distinctive.

All scientific names take the form of Latin words, though they may come from other languages and can even be words that the describer makes up. If they come from Chinese or some other language that is not written in the roman alphabet, they must be transliterated so that they can be treated according to the rules of Latin grammar. The genus name is a noun; the species name can be either an adjective, a noun in apposition (one that explains the generic name), or a noun in the genitive case (a possessive). If it is an adjective, it must agree in gender with the genus name; the adjectival ending must be changed if the species is transferred to another genus that is of a different gender. Usually adjectives that modify masculine nouns end in *-us,* those that modify feminine nouns end in *-a,* and those that modify neuter nouns end in *-um,* but there are other endings (for example, *-is,* and *-inne*).

Many scientific names are accompanied by the name of the describer and the date of the original description. These elements are not parts of the name but they can be useful. As you come to know something about natural history, the describer's name will conjure up images of the conditions of the time. The name Mitchill after a fish species name brings forth the image of Samuel Latham Mitchill, a blustery doctor-politician-naturalist from New York in the early nineteenth century. The name of David Starr Jordan, a true genius and the first president of Stanford University, recalls the man who dominated our science from 1870 to 1929.

There are no objective criteria as to what constitutes a genus (or any other category above the species level), so species are frequently shifted to other genera as new information about relationships comes to light. We then may have to change the adjectival ending. We place the name of the describer (and the date, if it is cited) in parentheses, to indicate that the species was originally assigned to a different genus.

Names of families always are formed by the addition of -idae to the root name of a genus, which is then called the type genus. Thus the family name Cyprinidae is based on the genus *Cyprinus,* and Percidae comes from *Perca* + -idae. The type genus is simply the one the describer of the family selected to represent the family, presumably because it was thought to be typical of the family.

A new species officially acquires a name when the name is published in a scientific paper that is generally available to anyone who is interested. The rules are quite specific about what constitutes publication (they specify, for example, that the description must be printed in ink on paper) and they require a description and a diagnosis that specifies how the new species differs from similar species.

But what if someone else has already discovered "your" species and published it in a journal that you were not aware of? The basic rule is that the name published first stands. Your name then becomes a junior synonym and the other name is the valid name (of which there can be only one at a time). If it is later discovered that the early name is not valid for some reason (perhaps it wasn't really the same species as yours), then your available name becomes the valid name. The idea is that each animal species can have only one name at a time, but in practice this seemingly simple objective can be very difficult to attain.

Some species vary from one part of their range to another. If there are two or more forms, each of which occurs over a considerable area with a narrow transitional zone between them, it may be desirable to name the forms as subspecies. Subspecies—really the basic evolutionary units—have three-word names. The northern longear sunfish, for example, is *Lepomis megalotis peltastes* Cope, 1870: genus *Lepomis*, species *megalotis*, subspecies *peltastes*, described by Edward Drinker Cope in 1870.

Nomenclature is the basis of communication about organisms and it does have a charm and romance all its own. In the following lists of words and word parts that appear frequently in fish names, L. stands for Latin, M.L. for Middle Latin, N.L. for New Latin, and Gr. for Greek.

Shape, Size

acus	(L.) a point
alt	(L.) high
anom	(Gr.) without law, irregular
brev	(L.) short
carin	(L.) a keel
elong	(L.) long (*e*, out or beyond, + *longus*, long)
falc	(L.) sickle, scythe
fus	(L.) spindle

gibb	(L.) bent, hunched
long	(L.) long
meg	(Gr.) great, large
micr	(Gr.) small
olig	(Gr.) few, small
oxy	(Gr.) sharp
platy	(Gr.) flat, broad
pygm	(L.) small, pygmy
robust	(L.). oaken, strong, robust

Color, Pattern

ater	(L.) black
aurat	(L.) rich in gold
brunne	(M.L.) dark brown
caerul	(L.) dark blue
chlor	(Gr.) green
cruent	(L.) bloody
cyan	(Gr.) dark blue
flav	(L.) yellow
fusc	(L.) dark brown
gutt	(L.) drop; spotted as with raindrops
lin	(L.) line
macul	(L.) spot or stain
nigr	(L.) dark, black
notat	(L.) marked
ocell	(L.) little eye; eyelike spot
plumb	(L.) lead
punct	(L.) sting or puncture; spotted as if punctured
ros	(L.) rose
rub	(L.) red
ruf	(L.) reddish
stell	(L.) star
stri	(L.) furrow or channel
umbros	(L.) shady
vari	(L.) variable, variegate
zon	(Gr.) girdle; (L.) banded

Structures

acanth	(Gr.) thorn, spine
arch	(Gr.) beginning; rectum
bucc	(L.) cheek
cephal	(Gr.) head
corn	(L.) horn
frons	(L.) forehead, brow
genys	(Gr.) cheek
lep	(Gr.) scale
lingu	(L.) tongue
ocul	(L.) eye
ophthalm	(Gr.) eye
ops	(Gr.) aspect, appearance
ot	(Gr.) ear
pinn	(L.) wing
pter	(Gr.) wing, fin
rostr	(L.) bill, snout
spin	(L.) thorn (spine)
stom	(Gr.) mouth
ur	(Gr.) tail
vel	(L.) veil, covering (sail)

General

aest	(L.) summer
all	(Gr.) other, strange
bi	(L.) two
ellus	(L.) diminutive ending
ensis	(L.) belonging to
eu	(Gr.) good, true
hetero	(Gr.) other, different
homo	(Gr.) common, alike, equal
ifer	(L.) *i* + *fer*, bearing
iform	(L.) *i* + *form*, shape
oides	(N.L.) likeness, form
sax	(L.) stone

Index

The color plates are located between pages 180 and 181.